KAPLAN PUBLISHING

CW01650468

THIS EXAM KIT COMES WITH
FREE ONLINE ACCESS
TO EXTRA RESOURCES AIMED AT HELPING YOU PASS YOUR EXAMS

IN ADDITION TO THE OFFICIAL QUESTIONS AND ANSWERS IN THIS BOOK, GO ONLINE AND EN-gage WITH:

- An iPaper version of the Exam Kit
- Articles including Key Examinable Areas
- Material updates
- Latest Official ACCA exam questions
- Extra question assistance using the Signpost icon
- Timed Questions with an online tutor debrief using the Clock icon

And you can access all of these extra resources anytime, anywhere using your EN-gage account.

How to access your online resources

If you are a Kaplan Financial tuition, full-time or distance learning student

You will already have an EN-gage account and these extra resources will be available to you online. You do not need to register again, as this process was completed when you enrolled. If having problems accessing online materials, please ask your course administrator.

If you purchased through Kaplan Flexible Learning or via the Kaplan Publishing website

You will automatically receive an e-mail invitation to EN-gage online. Please register your details using this e-mail to gain access to your content. If you do not receive the e-mail or book content, please contact our Technical Support team at engage@twinsystems.com.

If you are already a registered EN-gage user

Go to www.EN-gage.co.uk and log in. Select the 'add a book' feature and enter the ISBN number of this book and the unique pass key at the bottom of this card. Then click 'finished' or 'add another book'. You may add as many books as you have purchased from this screen.

If you are a new EN-gage user

Register at www.EN-gage.co.uk and click on the link contained in the e-mail we sent you to activate your account. Then select the 'add a book' feature, enter the ISBN number of this book and the unique pass key at the bottom of this card. Then click 'finished' or 'add another book'.

Your Code and Information

This code can only be used once for the registration of one book online. This registration will expire when the final sittings for the examinations covered by this book have taken place. Please allow one hour from the time you submitted your book details for us to process your request.

EN-gage

p1Vb-C3Pa-FeAb-hzR6

Please be aware that this code is case-sensitive and you will need to include the dashes within the passcode, but not when entering the ISBN. For further technical support, please visit www.EN-gage.co.uk

For technical support, please visit www.EN-gage.co.uk

Professional Examinations

Paper F3

Financial Accounting (INT)

EXAM KIT

KAPLAN PUBLISHING

British Library Cataloguing-in-Publication Data

A catalogue record for this book is available from the British Library.

Published by:

Kaplan Publishing UK

Unit 2 The Business Centre

Molly Millar's Lane

Wokingham

Berkshire

RG41 2QZ

ISBN: 978-1-84710-986-6

Printed in the UK by CPI William Clowes, Beccles, NR34 7TL.

Acknowledgements

The past ACCA examination questions are the copyright of the Association of Chartered Certified Accountants. The original answers to the questions from June 1994 onwards were produced by the examiners themselves and have been adapted by Kaplan Publishing.

We are grateful to the Chartered Institute of Management Accountants and the Institute of Chartered Accountants in England and Wales for permission to reproduce past examination questions. The answers have been prepared by Kaplan Publishing.

CONTENTS

NEW **New features in this edition**

In addition to providing a wide ranging bank of practice questions, we have also included in this edition:

- Paper specific information and advice on exam technique.
- Our recommended approach to make your revision for this particular subject as effective as possible.

  This includes step by step guidance on how best to use our Kaplan material (Complete text, pocket notes and exam kit) at this stage in your studies.
- Objective test questions section.

You will find a wealth of other resources to help you with your studies on the following sites:

www.EN-gage.co.uk and www.accaglobal.com/students/

INDEX TO QUESTIONS AND ANSWERS

PRACTICE QUESTIONS

EXAM TECHNIQUE

- **Do not skip any of the material** in the syllabus.
- **Read each question** *very* carefully.
- **Double-check your answer** before committing yourself to it.
- Answer **every** question – if you do not know an answer, you don't lose anything by guessing. Think carefully before you **guess**. The examiner has indicated that many candidates are still leaving blank answers in the real exam.
- If you are answering a multiple-choice question, **eliminate first those answers that you know are wrong**. Then choose the most appropriate answer from those that are left.
- Remember that **only one answer to a multiple-choice question can be right**. After you have eliminated the ones that you know to be wrong, if you are still unsure, guess. Only guess after you have double-checked that you have only eliminated answers that are *definitely* wrong.
- **Don't panic** if you realise you've answered a question incorrectly. Getting one question wrong will not mean the difference between passing and failing

Computer-based exams – tips

- Do not attempt a CBE until you have **completed all study material** relating to it.
- On the ACCA website there is a CBE demonstration. It is **ESSENTIAL** that you attempt this before your real CBE. You will become familiar with how to move around the CBE screens and the way that questions are formatted, increasing your confidence and speed in the actual exam.
- Be sure you understand how to use the **software** before you start the exam. If in doubt, ask the assessment centre staff to explain it to you.
- Questions are **displayed on the screen** and answers are entered using keyboard and mouse. At the end of the exam, you are given a certificate showing the result you have achieved.
- In addition to the traditional multiple-choice question type, CBEs might also contain **other types of questions**, such as number entry questions, formula entry questions, and stem questions with multiple parts. There are also questions that carry several marks.
- You need to be sure you **know how to answer questions** of this type before you sit the exam, through practice.

PAPER SPECIFIC INFORMATION

THE EXAM

FORMAT OF THE PAPER-BASED AND COMPUTER-BASED EXAM

	Number of marks
40 compulsory multiple-choice questions (2 marks each)	80
10 compulsory short-form questions (1 mark each)	10
Total time allowed: 2 hours	90

- In any exam there will be roughly 8 or 9 questions for **each** of the six main syllabus areas
- Two mark questions will usually comprise the following answer types:
  (i) Multiple choice with four options (A, B, C or D)
  (ii) Require you to enter a numerical answer (CBE only)
  (iii) Ask you to select two correct answers from a choice of four
- The one mark questions will predominately be theory questions and will comprise the following:
  (i) Multiple choice with either two or three options
  (ii) True or false options
  (iii) Yes or no options
- ACCA official statistics have shown that most students do not find the exam time pressured and that the 1 mark questions do not seem to be any easier than the 2 mark questions

PASS MARK

The pass mark for all ACCA Qualification examination papers is 50%.

DETAILED SYLLABUS

The detailed syllabus and study guide written by the ACCA can be found at:

www.accaglobal.com/students/

KAPLAN'S RECOMMENDED REVISION APPROACH

QUESTION PRACTICE IS THE KEY TO SUCCESS

Success in professional examinations relies upon you acquiring a firm grasp of the required knowledge at the tuition phase. In order to be able to do the questions, knowledge is essential.

However, the difference between success and failure often hinges on your exam technique on the day and making the most of the revision phase of your studies.

The **Kaplan complete text** is the starting point, designed to provide the underpinning knowledge to tackle all questions. However, in the revision phase, pouring over text books is not the answer.

Kaplan Online fixed tests help you consolidate your knowledge and understanding and are a useful tool to check whether you can remember key topic areas.

Kaplan pocket notes are designed to help you quickly revise a topic area, however you then need to practice questions. There is a need to progress to full exam standard questions as soon as possible, and to tie your exam technique and technical knowledge together.

The importance of question practice cannot be over-emphasised.

The recommended approach below is designed by expert tutors in the field, in conjunction with their knowledge of the examiner.

The approach taken for the fundamental papers is to revise by topic area.

You need to practice as many questions as possible in the time you have left.

OUR AIM

Our aim is to get you to the stage where you can attempt exam standard questions confidently, to time, in a closed book environment, with no supplementary help (i.e. to simulate the real examination experience).

Practising your exam technique on real past examination questions, in timed conditions, is also vitally important for you to assess your progress and identify areas of weakness that may need more attention in the final run up to the examination.

The approach below shows you which questions you should use to build up to coping with exam standard question practice, and references to the sources of information available should you need to revisit a topic area in more detail.

Remember that in the real examination, all you have to do is:

- attempt all questions required by the exam
- only spend the allotted time on each question, and
- get them at least 50% right!

Try and practice this approach on every question you attempt from now to the real exam.

THE KAPLAN PAPER F3 REVISION PLAN

Stage 1: Assess areas of strengths and weaknesses

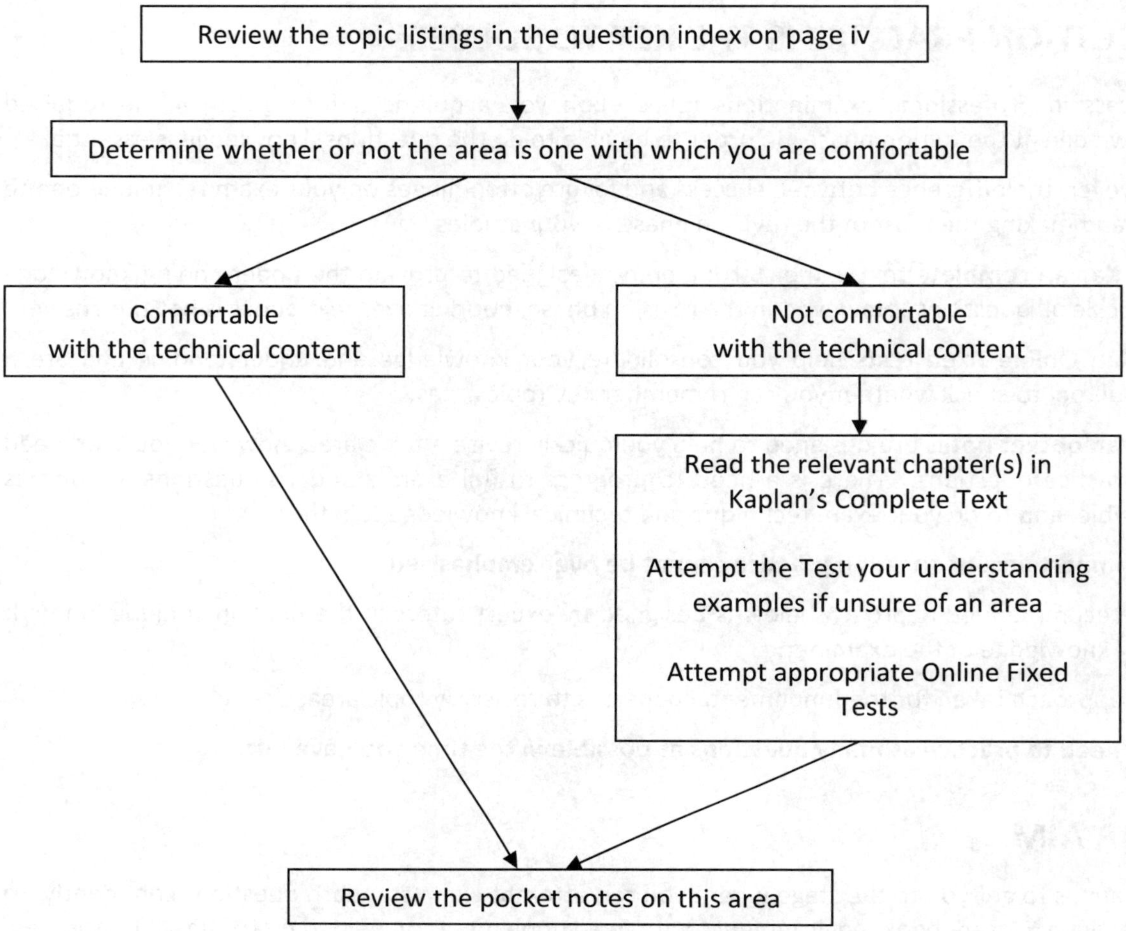

Stage 2: Practice questions

Ensure that you revise all syllabus areas as questions could be asked on anything.

Try to avoid referring to text books and notes and the model answer until you have completed your attempt.

Try to answer the question in the allotted time.

Review your attempt with the model answer. If you got the answer wrong, can you see why? Was the problem a lack of knowledge or a failure to understand the question fully?

Fill in the self-assessment box below and decide on your best course of action.

Comfortable with question attempt

↓

Only revisit when comfortable with questions on all topic areas

Not comfortable with question attempts

↓

Focus on these areas by:

- Reworking test your understanding examples in Kaplan's Complete Text
- Revisiting the technical content from Kaplan's pocket notes
- Working any remaining questions on that area in the exam kit

Stage 3: Final pre-exam revision

We recommend that you **attempt at least one two hour mock examination** containing a set of previously unseen exam standard questions.

It is important that you get a feel for the breadth of coverage of a real exam without advanced knowledge of the topic areas covered – just as you will expect to see on the real exam day.

Ideally this mock should be sat in timed, closed book, real exam conditions and could be:

- a mock examination offered by your tuition provider, and/or
- the pilot paper in the back of this exam kit, and/or
- the practice simulation paper in this kit

Section 1

PRACTICE QUESTIONS

INTRODUCTION TO ACCOUNTING

1 Which of the following statements is true?

A The directors of a company are liable for any losses of the company

B A sole trader business is owned by shareholders and operated by the proprietor

C Partners are liable for losses in a partnership in proportion to their profit share ratio

D A company is run by directors on behalf of its members **(2 marks)**

2 Which of the following best describes management accounts?

A Management accounts are mandatory accounts which reflect the past performance of a business and are prepared in accordance with strict accounting requirements

B Management accounts are normally prepared monthly on a rolling basis and include details of past performance as well as budgets and forecasts

C Management accounts are required by law and include sufficient detail for managers control the business and prepare for the future

D Management accounts include information computed to be relevant to managers and are generally prepared annually **(2 marks)**

3 Which of the following best explains why employees are interested in the financial statements of their employer?

A To compare the business with its competitors in order to decide whether to seek employment with one of those competitors

B To assess the effect of the business on the local economy, community and environment

C To assess whether the business will continue into the foreseeable future

D To assess the profitability of the business in order to decide whether to invest in it **(2 marks)**

4 Which of the following user groups require the most detailed financial information?

A The management

B Investors and potential investors

C Government agencies **(1 mark)**

5 Which of the following statements are true?

1 Accounting can be described as the recording and summarising of transactions.

2 Financial accounting describes the production of a statement of financial position and income statement for internal use.

A 1 only

B 2 only **(1 mark)**

6 The main aim of financial accounting is to:

A record all transactions in the books of account

B provide management with detailed analyses of costs

C present the financial results to the organisation by means of recognised statements

D calculate profit **(2 marks)**

7 Which one of the following sentences does NOT explain the distinction between financial accounts and management accounts?

A Financial accounts are primarily for external users and management accounts are primarily for internal users

B Financial accounts are normally produced annually and management accounts are normally produced monthly

C Financial accounts are more accurate than management accounts

D Financial accounts are audited by an external auditor and management accounts do not normally have an external audit **(2 marks)**

STATEMENT OF FINANCIAL POSITION AND INCOME STATEMENT

8 The following information relates to Minnie's hairdressing business in the year ended 31 August 20X7:

	$
Expenses	7,100
Opening inventory	1,500
Closing inventory	900
Purchases	12,950
Gross profit	12,125
Inventory drawings of shampoo	75

What is the sales figure for the business?

A $32,700

B $25,600

C $25,675

D $25,750 **(2 marks)**

9 An asset is:

A An item owned by an entity

B An item controlled by an entity **(1 mark)**

10 Arthur had net assets of $19,000 at 30 April 20X7. During the year to 30 April 20X7, he introduced $9,800 additional capital into the business. Profits were $8,000, of which he withdrew $4,200.

What was the balance on Arthur's capital account at 1 May 20X6?

A $5,400

B $13,000

C $16,600

D $32,600 **(2 marks)**

11 The capital of a business would change as a result of:

A a supplier being paid by cheque

B raw materials being purchased on credit

C non-current assets being purchased on credit

D wages being paid in cash **(2 marks)**

12 A draft statement of financial position has been prepared for Lollipop, a sole trader. It is now discovered that a loan due for repayment by Lollipop fourteen months after the reporting date has been included in trade payables.

The necessary adjustment will:

A have no effect on net current assets

B increase net current assets

C reduce net current assets

D increase current assets but reduce net current assets **(2 marks)**

13 The profit of a business may be calculated by using which one of the following formulae?

A Opening capital – drawings + capital introduced – closing capital

B Closing capital + drawings – capital introduced – opening capital

C Opening capital + drawings – capital introduced – closing capital

D Closing capital – drawings + capital introduced – opening capital **(2 marks)**

14 Which accounting concept requires that amounts of goods taken from inventory by the proprietor of a business are treated as drawings?

A Accruals

B Prudence

C Separate entity

D Substance over form **(2 marks)**

15 The following information is available about Andrew's business at 30 September 20X6:

	$
Motor van	14,000
Loan (repayable in 4 equal annual installments starting 1 January 20X7)	100,000
Receivables	23,800
Bank balance (a debit on the bank statement)	3,250
Provision for depreciation	7,000
Payables	31,050
Inventory	12,560
Petty cash	150
Rent due	1,200
Allowance for receivables	1,500

What are the correct figures for current liabilities and current assets?

	Current liabilities	*Current assets*
	$	$
A	34,300	35,010
B	32,250	38,260
C	57,250	38,260
D	60,500	35,010

(2 marks)

16 The following transactions relate to Max's business:

1 May	Purchase of goods for resale on credit	$300
2 May	Max injects long term capital into the business	$1,400
3 May	Payment of rent made	$750
5 May	Max withdraws cash from the business	$400
7 May	Sales made on credit	$1,200

(goods originally cost $600)

At the start of the week, the assets of the business were $15,700 and liabilities amounted to $11,200.

At the end of the week, what is the amount of Max's capital ?

A $5,350

B $1,400

C $850

D $1,000 **(2 marks)**

DOUBLE ENTRY BOOKKEEPING

17 Oscar runs a sole trader business selling computers. On 12 January 20X7, he employed his daughter as an administrator for the business and took a computer from the store room for her to use in the office.

What is the double entry for this transaction?

A	Dr Drawings	Cr Cost of sales
B	Dr Non-current assets	Cr Cost of sales
C	Dr Cost of sales	Cr Drawings
D	Dr Cost of sales	Cr Non-current assets

(2 marks)

18 Which of the following items appear on the same side of the trial balance?

A Drawings and accruals

B Carriage outwards and prepayments

C Carriage inwards and rental income

D Opening inventory and purchase returns **(2 marks)**

19 The double-entry system of book-keeping normally results in which of the following balances on the ledger accounts?

	Debit balances:	*Credit balances:*
A	Assets and revenues	Liabilities, capital and expenses
B	Revenues, capital and liabilities	Assets and expenses
C	Assets and expenses	Liabilities, capital and revenues
D	Assets, expenses and capital	Liabilities and revenues

(2 marks)

20 The most important reason for producing a trial balance prior to preparing the final accounts is:

A it confirms the accuracy of the ledger accounts

B it provides all the figures necessary to prepare the final accounts

C it shows that the ledger accounts contain debit and credit entries of an equal value

D it enables the accountant to calculate any adjustments required **(2 marks)**

21 Sasha has prepared a draft income statement for her business:

	$	$
Sales		256,800
Cost of sales		
Opening inventory	13,400	
Purchases	145,000	
Closing inventory	14,200	
		(144,200)
Gross profit		112,600
Expenses		(76,000)
Net profit		36,600

Sasha has not yet recorded the following items:

- Carriage in of $2,300
- Discounts received of $3,900
- Discounts allowed of $1,950

After these amounts are recorded, what are the revised gross and net profits of Sasha's business?

	Gross profit $	*Net profit* $
A	108,350	36,250
B	108,350	28,450
C	110,300	28,450
D	110,300	36,250

(2 marks)

22 Elijah started the month with a positive balance of $1,780 on his bank account. What is the balance after the following transactions in June?

1 Elijah withdraws $200 per week to cover living expenses.

2 A settlement discount of $30 is taken by a customer on a sale of $600.

3 An amount of $400 is received from a credit customer.

4 Bankings of $1,200 from petty cash.

A $3,750

B $3,150

C $3,180

D $2,580

(2 marks)

23 After corrections, what should be the balance on the following account?

Bank

	$		$
Overdraft at start of month	1,340	Returns of goods purchased for cash	50
Reimbursement of petty cash float	45	Payments to credit suppliers	990
Receipts from customers	4,400	Rental income	1,300
		Payment of electricity bill	700
		Balance c/f	2,745
	5,785		5,785

A $2,665

B $2,765

C $5,345

D $2,675 **(2 marks)**

24 Andrea started a taxi business by transferring her car, worth $5,000, into the business.

What are the accounting entries required to record this?

A Dr Capital $5,000, Cr Car $5,000

B Dr Car $5,000, Cr Drawings $5,000

C Dr Car $5,000, Cr Capital $5,000 **(1 mark)**

INVENTORY

25 An item of inventory was purchased for $500. It is expected to be sold for $1,200 although $250 will need to be spent on it in order to achieve the sale. To replace the same item of inventory would cost $650. How should the inventory be valued in the accounts?

A $500

B $750

C $950

D $650 **(2 marks)**

26 Appleby buys and sells inventory during the month of August as follows:

Opening inventory		100 units	$2.52/unit
4 August	Sales	20 units	
8 August	Purchases	140 units	$2.56/unit
10 August	Sales	90 units	
18 August	Purchases	200 units	$2.78/unit
20 August	Sales	180 units	

The periodic weighted average for the month is calculated as follows:

Total value of inventory (opening inventory plus purchase costs during the month) divided by total units (opening inventory plus purchase costs during the month).

Which of the following statements is true?

A Closing inventory is $19.50 higher when using the FIFO method instead of the periodic weighted average

B Closing inventory is $19.50 lower when using the FIFO method instead of the periodic weighted average

C Closing inventory is $17.50 higher when using the FIFO method instead of the periodic weighted average

D Closing inventory is $17.50 lower when using the FIFO method instead of the periodic weighted average **(2 marks)**

27 In the year ended 31 August 20X4, Aplus' records show closing inventory of 1,000 units compared to 950 units of opening inventory. Which of the following statements is true assuming that prices have fallen throughout the year?

A Closing inventory and profit are higher using FIFO rather than AVCO.

B Closing inventory and profit are lower using FIFO rather than AVCO.

C Closing inventory is higher and profit lower using FIFO rather than AVCO.

D Closing inventory is lower and profit higher using FIFO rather than AVCO.

(2 marks)

28 David performs an inventory count on 30 December 20X6 ahead of the 31 December year end. He counts 1,200 identical units, each of which cost $50. On 31 December, David sold 20 of the units for $48 each. What figure should be included in David's statement of financial position for inventory at the year end?

A $60,000

B $59,000

C $57,600

D $56,640 **(2 marks)**

29 Which of the following statements about the treatment of inventory and work in progress in financial statements are correct?

(1) Inventory should be valued at the lower of cost, net realisable value and replacement cost.

(2) In valuing work in progress, materials costs, labour costs and variable and fixed production overheads must be included.

(3) Inventory items can be valued using either first in, first out (FIFO) or weighted average cost.

(4) A company's financial statements must disclose the accounting policies used in measuring inventories.

A All four statements are correct

B 1, 2 and 3 only

C 2, 3 and 4 only

D 1 and 4 only **(2 marks)**

30 Kiera's interior design business received a delivery of fabric on 29 June 20X6, which was included in inventory at 30 June 20X6. The invoice for the goods was recorded in July 20X6.

What effect will this have on the business?

1 Profit for the year ended 30 June 20X6 will be overstated.

2 Inventory at 30 June 20X6 will be understated.

3 Profit for the year ended 30 June 20X7 will be overstated.

4 Inventory at 30 June 20X6 will be overstated.

A 1 and 2

B 2 and 3

C 1 only

D 1 and 4 **(2 marks)**

31 What journal entry is required to record goods taken from inventory by the owner of a business?

A	Dr Drawings	Cr Purchases
B	Dr Sales	Cr Drawings
C	Dr Drawings	Cr Inventory

(1 mark)

32 A business had an opening inventory of $180,000 and a closing inventory of $220,000 in its financial statements for the year ended 31 December 20X5.

Which of the following entries for these opening and closing inventory figures are made when completing the financial records of the business?

		Debit $	Credit $
A	Inventory account	180,000	
	Income statement		180,000
	Income statement	220,000	
	Inventory account		220,000
B	Income statement	180,000	
	Inventory account		180,000
	Inventory account	220,000	
	Income statement		220,000
C	Inventory account	40,000	
	Purchases account		40,000
D	Purchases account	40,000	
	Inventory account		40,000

(2 marks)

33 Ajay's annual inventory count took place on 7 July 20X6. The inventory value on this date was $38,950. During the period from 30 June 20X6 to 7 July 20X6, the following took place:

Sales	$6,500
Purchases	$4,250

The mark up is 25% on cost.

What is Ajay's inventory value at 30 June 20X6?

A $38,000

B $39,900

C $41,200

D $39,575

(2 marks)

34 Inventory movements for product X during the last quarter were as follows:

January	Purchases	10 items at $19.80 each
February	Sales	10 items at $30 each
March	Purchases	20 items at $24.50
	Sales	5 items at $30 each

Opening inventory at 1 January was 6 items valued at $15 each.

Gross profit for the quarter, using the continuous weighted average cost method, would be:

A $135.75

B $155.00

C $174.00

D $483.00 **(2 marks)**

35 Your firm values inventory using the weighted average cost method. At 1 October 20X8, there were 60 units in inventory valued at $12 each. On 8 October, 40 units were purchased for $15 each, and a further 50 units were purchased for $18 each on 14 October. On 21 October, 75 units were sold for $1,200.

The value of closing inventory at 31 October 20X8 was:

A $900

B $1,020

C $1,110

D $1,125 **(2 marks)**

36 Percy Pilbeam is a book wholesaler. On each sale, commission of 4% is payable to the selling agent.

The following information is available in respect of total inventories of three of his most popular titles at his financial year-end:

	Cost	*Selling price*
	$	$
Henry VII – Shakespeare	2,280	2,900
Dissuasion – Jane Armstrong-Siddeley	4,080	4,000
Pilgrim's Painful Progress – John Bunion	1,280	1,300

What is the total value of these inventories in Percy's statement of financial position?

A $7,368

B $7,400

C $7,560

D $7,640 **(2 marks)**

37 An organisation's inventory at 1 July is 15 units at $3.00 each. The following movements occur:

3 July 20X4 5 units sold at $3.30 each

8 July 20X4 10 units bought at $3.50 each

12 July 20X4 8 units sold at $4.00 each

Closing inventory at 31 July, using the FIFO method of inventory valuation, would be

A $31.50

B $36.00

C $39.00

D $41.00 **(2 marks)**

38 What would be the effect on a company's profit of discovering inventory with cost of $1,250 and a net realisable value of $1,000, assuming that the same inventory had not been included in the original inventory count?

A An increase of $1,250

B An increase of $1,000

C A decrease of $250

D No effect at all **(2 marks)**

39 S & Co sell three products – Basic, Super and Luxury. The following information was available at the year end:

	Basic	*Super*	*Luxury*
	$ per unit	$ per unit	$ per unit
Original cost	6	9	18
Estimated selling price	9	12	15
Selling and distribution costs	1	4	5
	units	units	units
Units in inventory	200	250	150

The value of inventory at the year end should be:

A $4,200

B $4,700

C $5,700

D $6,150 **(2 marks)**

40 In times of rising prices, the valuation of inventory using the First In First Out method, as opposed to the Weighted Average Cost method, will result in which ONE of the following combinations?

	Cost of sales	*Profit*	*Closing inventory*
A	Lower	Higher	Higher
B	Lower	Higher	Lower
C	Higher	Lower	Higher
D	Higher	Higher	Lower

(2 marks)

SALES TAX

41 Erin is registered for sales tax. During May, she sells goods with a tax exclusive price of $600 to Kyle on credit. As Kyle is buying a large quantity of goods, Erin reduces the price by 5%. She also offers a discount of another 3% if Kyle pays within 10 days. Kyle does not pay within the 10 days.

If sales tax is charged at 17.5%, what amount should Erin charge on this transaction?

A $96.76

B $101.85

C $99.75

D $105.00 **(2 marks)**

42 At 1 December 20X5, Laurel owes the authorities $23,778. During the month of December, she recorded the following transactions:

- Sales of $800,000 exclusive of 17.5% sales tax.
- Purchases of $590,790 inclusive of sales tax.

What is the balance on Laurel's sales tax account at the end of December?

A $54,937

B $60,389

C $75,788

D $163,778 **(2 marks)**

43 If Sales (including sales tax) amounted to $27,612.50, and Purchases (excluding sales tax) amounted to $18,000, the balance on the sales tax account, assuming all items are subject to tax at 17.5%, would be:

A $962.50 Dr

B $962.50 Cr

C $1,682.10 Dr

D $1,682.10 Cr **(2 marks)**

44 **In the quarter ended 31 March 20X2, Chas had taxable sales, net of sales tax, of $90,000 and taxable purchases, net of sales tax, of $72,000.**

If the rate of sales tax is 10%, how much sales tax is due?

A $1,800 receivable

B $2,000 receivable

C $1,800 payable

D $2,000 payable **(2 marks)**

45 **A summary of the transactions of Ramsgate, who is registered for sales tax at 17.5%, shows the following for the month of August 20X9.**

Outputs	$60,000 (exclusive of tax)
Inputs	$40,286 (inclusive of tax)

At the beginning of the period Ramsgate owed $3,400 to the authorities, and during the period he has paid $2,600 to them.

At the end of the period the amount owing to the authorities is:

A $3,700

B $3,930

C $4,400

D $5,300. **(2 marks)**

46 **The sales account is:**

A credited with the total of sales made, including sales tax

B credited with the total of sales made, excluding sales tax **(1 mark)**

47 **A business sold goods that had a net value of $600 to Lucid. What entries are required to record this transaction if sales tax is payable at 17.5%?**

A Dr Lucid $600, Dr Sales tax $105, Cr Sales $705

B Dr Lucid $705, Cr Sales tax $105, Cr Sales $600

C Dr Lucid $600, Cr Sales tax $105, Cr Sales $600

D Dr Sales $600, Dr Sales tax $105, Cr Lucid $705 **(2 marks)**

48 **Laker returned goods that had a net value of $200. What entries are required to record this transaction if sales tax is payable at 17.5%?**

A Dr Returns inward $200, Dr Sales tax $35, Cr Laker $235

B Dr Returns inward $235, Cr Sales tax $35, Cr Laker $200

C Dr Purchases $200, Dr Sales tax $35, Cr Laker $235

D Dr Laker $235, Cr Returns inward $200, Cr Sales tax $35 **(2 marks)**

49 Stung, which is registered for the purposes of sales tax, bought furniture on credit terms at a cost of $8,000, plus tax of $1,200.

What is the correct account entry?

		$
A	Furniture	9,200
	Supplier	9,200
B	Furniture	8,000
	Sales tax	1,200
	Supplier	6,800
C	Furniture	8,000
	Sales tax	1,200
	Supplier	9,200
D	Furniture	8,000
	Supplier	8,000

(2 marks)

50 Which of the following statements are true?

1 Sales tax is a form of indirect taxation.

2 If input tax exceeds output tax the difference is payable to the authorities.

3 Sales tax is included in the reported sales and purchases of the business.

4 Sales tax cannot be recovered on some purchases.

A 1 and 4

B 1 and 2

C 2 and 3

D 3 and 4 **(2 marks)**

ACCRUALS AND PREPAYMENTS

51 Leddley owns two properties which it rents to tenants. In the year ended 31 December 20X6, it received $280,000 in respect of property 1 and $160,000 in respect of property 2. Balances on the rental accounts were as follows:

	31 December 20X6	*31 December 20X5*
Property 1	13,400 Dr	12,300 Cr
Property 2	6,700 Cr	5,400 Dr

What amount should be credited to the income statement for the year ended 31 December 20X6 in respect of rental income?

A $453,600

B $440,200

C $465,900

D $475,600 **(2 marks)**

52 Troy, a property company, received cash totalling $838,600 from tenants during the year ended 31 December 20X6.

Figures for rent in advance and in arrears at the beginning and end of the year were:

	31 December 20X5	*31 December 20X6*
	$	$
Rent received in advance	102,600	88,700
Rent in arrears (all subsequently received)	42,300	48,400

What amount should appear in the company's income statement for the year ended 31 December 20X6 for rental income?

A $818,600

B $738,000

C $939,200

D $858,600 **(2 marks)**

53 Details of Bartlett's insurance policy are shown below:

Premium for year ended 31 March 20X6 paid April 20X5	$10,800
Premium for year ending 31 March 20X7 paid April 20X6	$12,000

What figures should be included in the company's financial statements for the year ended 30 June 20X6?

	Income statement	*Statement of financial position*
	$	$
A	11,100	9,000 prepayment
B	11,700	9,000 prepayment
C	11,100	9,000 accrual
D	11,700	9,000 accrual

(2 marks)

54 Vine sublets part of its office accommodation.

The rent is received quarterly in advance on 1 January, 1 April, 1 July and 1 October. The annual rent has been $24,000 for some years, but it was increased to $30,000 from 1 July 20X5.

What amounts for rent should appear in the company's financial statements for the year ended 31 January 20X6?

	Income statement	*Statement of financial position*
A	$27,500	$5,000 in accrued income
B	$27,000	$2,500 in accrued income
C	$27,000	$2,500 in prepaid income
D	$27,500	$5,000 in prepaid income

(2 marks)

55 At 1 September, the motor expenses account showed 4 months' insurance prepaid of $80 and petrol accrued of $95. During September, the outstanding petrol bill is paid, plus further bills of $245. At 30 September there is a further outstanding petrol bill of $120.

The amount to be shown in the income statement for motor expenses for September is:

A $385

B $415

C $445

D $460 **(2 marks)**

56 On 1 May 20X0, A pays a rent bill of $1,800 for the period to 30 April 20X1. What is the charge to the income statement and the entry in the statement of financial position for the year ended 30 November 20X0?

A $1,050 charge to income statement and prepayment of $750 in the statement of financial position

B $1,050 charge to income statement and accrual of $750 in the statement of financial position

C $1,800 charge to income statement and no entry in the statement of financial position

D $750 charge to income statement and prepayment of $1,050 in the statement of financial position

(2 marks)

57 The electricity account for the year ended 30 June 20X3 was as follows:

	$
Opening balance for electricity accrued at 1 July 20X2	300
Payments made during the year:	
1 August 20X2 for three months to 31 July 20X2	600
1 November 20X2 for three months to 31 October 20X2	720
1 February 20X3 for three months to 31 January 20X3	900
30 June 20X3 for three months to 30 April 20X3	840

Which of the following is the appropriate entry for electricity?

	Accrued at June 20X3	*Charged to income statement, year ended 30 June 20X3*
A	$Nil	$3,060
B	$460	$3,320
C	$560	$3,320
D	$560	$3,420

(2 marks)

58 **The annual insurance premium for S for the period 1 July 20X3 to 30 June 20X4 is $13,200, which is 10% more than the previous year. Insurance premiums are paid on 1 July.**

What is the income statement charge for insurance for the year ended 31 December 20X3?

A $11,800

B $12,540

C $12,600

D $13,200 **(2 marks)**

59 **Farthing's year-end is 30 September. On 1 January 20X6 the organisation took out a loan of $100,000 with annual interest of 12%. The interest is payable in equal instalments on the first day of April, July, October and January in arrears.**

How much should be charged to the income statement account for the year ended 30 September 20X6, and how much should be accrued on the statement of financial position?

	Income statement	*Statement of financial position*
A	$12,000	$3,000
B	$9,000	$3,000
C	$9,000	Nil
D	$6,000	$3,000

(2 marks)

60 **On the first day of Month 1, a business had prepaid insurance of $10,000. On the first day of Month 8, it paid, in full, the annual insurance invoice of $36,000, to cover the following year.**

The amount charged in the income statement and the amount shown in the statement of financial position at the year-end is:

	Income statement $	*Balance carried forward* $
A	5,000	24,000
B	22,000	23,000
C	25,000	21,000
D	36,000	15,000

(2 marks)

61 **Which of the following statements is not true?**

A Accruals decrease profit

B Accrued income decreases profit

C A prepayment is an asset **(1 mark)**

IRRECOVERABLE DEBTS AND ALLOWANCES FOR RECEIVABLES

62 The following balances relate to Putney:

	$
Receivables at 1.1.X8	34,500
Cash received from credit customers	229,900
Contra with payables	1,200
Discounts allowed	17,890
Cash sales	24,000
Irrecoverable debts	18,600
Increase in allowance for receivables	12,500
Discounts received	15,670
Receivables at 31.12.X8	45,000

What is the revenue figure reported by Putney in the year ended 31 December 20X8?

A $275,870

B $278,090

C $290,590

D $302,090 **(2 marks)**

63 The following account has been extracted from the nominal ledger of Purdey:

Receivables ledger control account

	$		$
Balance b/f	84,700		
Contra with payables ledger control account	5,000	Irrecoverable debts	4,300
Discounts received	21,100	Discounts allowed	30,780
Credit sales	644,000	Cash received from credit customers	595,000
Cash sales	13,500	Increase in allowance for receivables	6,555
		Balance c/f	131,665
	768,300		768,300

After corrections, what is the receivables balance?

A $103,300

B $93,620

C $103,620

D $87,065 **(2 marks)**

64 Newell's receivables ledger control account shows a balance at the end of the year of $58,200 before making the following adjustments:

(i) Newell wishes to write off debts amounting to $8,900 as he believes they are irrecoverable.

(ii) He also wishes to make specific allowance for Carroll's debt of $1,350 and Juff's debt of $750.

(iii) He wishes to maintain a general allowance of 3% of the year end receivables balance.

Newell's allowance for receivables at the last year end was $5,650.

What is the charge to the income statement in respect of the above?

A $6,766

B $11,034

C $6,829

D $10,971 **(2 marks)**

65 In the statement of financial position at 31 December 20X5, Boris reported net receivables of $12,000. During 20X6 he made sales on credit of $125,000 and received cash from credit customers amounting to $115,500. At 31 December 20X6, Boris wished to write off debts of $7,100 and increase the allowance for receivables by $950 to $2,100. What is the net receivables figure at 31 December 20X6?

A $12,300

B $13,450

C $14,400

D $15,550 **(2 marks)**

66 At 1 July 20X5, a company's allowance for receivables was $48,000.

At 30 June 20X6, trade receivables amounted to $838,000. It was decided to write off $72,000 of these debts and adjust the allowance for receivables to $60,000.

What are the final amounts for inclusion in the company's statement of financial position at 30 June 20X6?

	Trade receivables	*Allowance for receivables*	*Net balance*
	$	$	$
A	838,000	60,000	778,000
B	766,000	60,000	706,000
C	766,000	108,000	658,000
D	838,000	108,000	730,000

(2 marks)

67 **In the year ended 30 September 20X8, Fauntleroy had sales of $7,000,000. Year end receivables amounted to 5% of annual sales. Fauntleroy wishes to maintain the allowance for receivables at 4% of receivables and as a result discovers that the allowance is 20% higher than at the previous year end.**

During the year irrecoverable debts amounting to $3,200 were written off and debts amounting to $450 and previously written off were recovered.

What is the irrecoverable debt expense for the year?

A $5,083

B $5,550

C $5,583

D $16,750 **(2 marks)**

68 **On 1 January 20X3 Tipton's trade receivables were $10,000. The following relates to the year ended 31 December 20X3:**

	$
Credit sales	100,000
Cash receipts	90,000
Discounts allowed	800
Discounts received	700

Cash receipts include $1,000 in respect of a receivable previously written off.

On 31 December 20X3 receivables were:

A $20,200

B $19,300

C $20,800

D $20,700 **(2 marks)**

69 **A company has been notified that a customer has been declared bankrupt. The company had previously provided for this doubtful debt. Which of the following is the correct double entry?**

	Dr	*Cr*
A	Irrecoverable debts account	The customer
B	The customer	Irrecoverable debts account
C	Allowance for receivables	The customer

(1 mark)

70 Headington is owed $37,500 by its customers at the start, and $39,000 at the end, of its year ended 31 December 20X8.

During the period, cash sales of $263,500 and credit sales of $357,500 were made, discounts allowed amounted to $15,750 and discounts received $21,400. Irrecoverable debts of $10,500 were written off and Headington wishes to retain its allowance for receivables at 5% of total receivables.

The cash received from receivables in the year totalled:

A $329,750

B $593,175

C $593,250

D $614,650 **(2 marks)**

71 The sales revenue in a company was $2 million and its receivables were 5% of sales. The company wishes to have an allowance for receivables of 4% of receivables, which would make the allowance one-third higher than the current allowance.

How will the profit for the period be affected by the change in allowance?

A Profit will be reduced by $1,000

B Profit will be increased by $1,000

C Profit will be reduced by $1,333

D Profit will be increased by $1,333 **(2 marks)**

72 A company started the year with total receivables of $87,000 and an allowance for receivables of $2,500.

During the year, two specific debts were written off, one for $800 and the other for $550. A debt of $350 that had been written off as irrecoverable in the previous year was paid during the year. At the year end, total receivables were $90,000 and the allowance for receivables was $2,300.

What is the charge to the income statement for the year in respect of irrecoverable and doubtful debts?

A $800

B $1,000

C $1,150

D $1,550 **(2 marks)**

73 An increase in the allowance for receivables results in:

A an increase in net current assets

B a decrease in net current assets **(1 mark)**

74 At the end of 20X7, Chester's receivable's balance is $230,000. He wishes to make specific allowance for Emily's debt of $450 and Lulu's debt of $980. He also wishes to maintain a general allowance of 5% of receivables.

What amount should be charged or credited to the income statement in respect of the allowance if the allowance at the start of the year was $11,700?

A $1,159 Dr

B $1,230 Dr

C $200 Cr

D $12,930 Dr **(2 marks)**

75 Which of the following is not a benefit of providing credit to customers?

A May result in increased sales

B Encourages customer loyalty

C Attracts new customers

D Improves the cash flow of the business **(2 marks)**

76 Which of the following best explains the purpose of an aged receivables analysis?

A To ensure that credit is not extended to unapproved customers or those that in the past have not paid

B To ensure that credit does not exceed agreed limits

C To keep track of outstanding debts and follow up those that are overdue **(1 mark)**

NON-CURRENT ASSETS

77 The asset register shows a carrying value for non-current assets of $85,600; the ledger accounts include a cost balance of $185,000 and an accumulated depreciation balance of $55,000. Which of the following may explain the discrepancy?

A The omission of an addition of land costing $30,000 from the ledger account and the omission of the disposal of an asset from the register (cost $25,600 and accumulated depreciation at disposal $11,200)

B The omission of the revaluation of an asset upwards by $16,600 and the depreciation charge of $20,000 from the ledger account and the omission of the disposal of an asset with carrying value $41,000 from the register

C The omission of the disposal of an asset from the ledger accounts (cost $25,600 and accumulated depreciation at disposal $11,200) and the omission of an addition of land costing $30,000 from the register.

D The omission of an upwards revaluation by $16,400 from the register and the accidental debiting of the depreciation charge of $28,000 to the accumulated depreciation ledger account **(2 marks)**

78 Laurie bought an asset on the 1st January 20X4 for $235,000. He has depreciated it at 30% using the reducing balance method. On 1st January 20X7, Laurie revalued the asset to $300,000.

What double entry should Laurie post to record the revaluation?

A	Dr Non-current assets cost	$65,000	Cr Revaluation reserve	$219,395
	Dr Accumulated depreciation	$154,395		
B	Dr Non-current assets cost	$65,000	Cr Revaluation reserve	$276,500
	Dr Accumulated depreciation	$211,500		
C	Dr Revaluation reserve	$219,395	Cr Non-current assets cost	$65,000
			Cr Accumulated depreciation	$154,395
D	Dr Revaluation reserve	$276,500	Cr Non-current assets cost	$65,000
			Cr Accumulated depreciation	$211,500

(2 marks)

79 A non-current asset register is:

A an alternative name for the non-current asset ledger account

B a list of the physical non-current assets rather than their financial cost

C a schedule of planned maintenance of non-current assets for use by the plant engineer

D a schedule of the cost and other information about each individual non-current asset

(1 mark)

80 IAS 16 Property, plant and equipment requires non-current assets to start being depreciated when

A They are available for normal use

B They are being used normally

C They are purchased **(1 mark)**

81 The plant and equipment account in the records of a company for the year ended 31 December 20X6 is shown below:

Plant and equipment – cost

	$		$
Balance b/f	960,000		
1 July Cash	48,000	30 Sept Disposals	84,000
		Balance c/f	924,000
	1,008,000		1,008,000

The company's policy is to charge straight line depreciation at 20% per year on a pro rata basis.

What should be the charge for depreciation in the company's income statement for the year ended 31 December 20X6?

A $184,800

B $192,600

C $191,400

D $184,200 **(2 marks)**

82 On 1 January 20X7, a company purchased some plant.

The invoice showed:

	$
Cost of plant	48,000
Delivery to factory	400
One year warranty covering breakdown	800
	49,200

Modifications to the factory building costing $2,200 were necessary to enable the plant to be installed.

What amount should be capitalised for the plant in the company's records?

A $51,400

B $48,000

C $50,600

D $48,400 **(2 marks)**

83 A non-current asset was purchased at the beginning of Year 1 for $2,400 and depreciated by 20% per annum using the reducing balance method. At the beginning of Year 4 it was sold for $1,200. The result of this was:

A a loss on disposal of $240.00

B a loss on disposal of $28.80

C a profit on disposal of $28.80

D a profit on disposal of $240.00 **(2 marks)**

84 A business' non-current assets had a book value of $125,000. An asset which had cost $12,000 was sold for $9,000, at a profit of $2,000.

What is the revised book value of non-current assets?

A $113,000

B $118,000

C $125,000

D $127,000 **(2 marks)**

85 W bought a new printing machine from abroad. The cost of the machine was $80,000. The installation costs were $5,000 and the employees received specific training on how to use this particular machine, at a cost of $2,000. Before using the machine to print customers' orders, a test was undertaken which used up paper and ink costing $1,000.

What should be the cost of the machine in the company's statement of financial position?

A $80,000

B $85,000

C $86,000

D $88,000 **(2 marks)**

86 A non-current asset was disposed of for $2,200 during the last accounting year. It had been purchased exactly three years earlier for $5,000, with an expected residual value of $500, and had been depreciated on the reducing balance basis, at 20% per annum.

The gain or loss on disposal was:

A $360 loss

B $150 loss

C $104 loss

D $200 profit **(2 marks)**

87 At the end of its financial year, Tanner has the following non-current assets:

Land and buildings at cost	$10.4 million
Land and buildings: accumulated depreciation	$0.12 million

The company has decided to revalue its land and buildings at the year end to $15 million.

What will be the amount of the adjustment on revaluation?

A $4.48m

B $4.6m

C $4.72m

D $15.12m **(2 marks)**

88 Which one of the following should be accounted for as capital expenditure?

A The cost of painting a building

B The replacement of windows in a building

C The purchase of a car by a garage for re-sale

D Legal fees incurred on the purchase of a building **(2 marks)**

89 A car was purchased for $12,000 on 1 April 20X1 and has been depreciated at 20% each year straight line, assuming no residual value.

The company policy is to charge a full year's depreciation in the year of purchase and no depreciation in the year of sale. The car was traded in for a replacement vehicle on 1 August 20X4 for an agreed figure of $5,000.

What was the profit or loss on the disposal of the vehicle for the year ended 31 December 20X4?

A Loss $2,200

B Loss $1,400

C Loss $200

D Profit $200 **(2 marks)**

90 At 30 September 20X2, the following balances existed in the records of Lambda:

Plant and equipment:

Cost	$860,000
Accumulated depreciation	$397,000

During the year ended 30 September 20X3, plant with a written down value of $37,000 was sold for $49,000. The plant had originally cost $80,000. Plant purchased during the year cost $180,000. It is the company's policy to charge a full year's depreciation in the year of acquisition of an asset and none in the year of sale, using a rate of 10% on the straight line basis.

What net amount should appear in Lambda's statement of financial position at 30 September 20X3 for plant and equipment?

A $563,000

B $467,000

C $510,000

D $606,000 **(2 marks)**

91 Depreciation is best described as:

A a means of spreading the payment for non-current assets over a period of years

B a decline in the market value of the assets

C a means of spreading the net cost of non-current assets over their estimated useful life

D a means of estimating the amount of money needed to replace the assets **(2 marks)**

92 **On 1 January 20X8, Wootton has a building in its books at cost $380,000, net book value $260,000.**

On 1 July 20X8, the asset is revalued at $450,000 and Wootton wishes to include that valuation in its books. Wootton's accounting policy is to depreciate buildings at 3% straight line.

The depreciation charge to the income statement for the year ended 31 Dec is:

A $8,300

B $11,400

C $12,450

D $13,500 **(2 marks)**

93 **A car was purchased by a newsagent business in May 20X1 for:**

	$
Cost	10,000
Road tax	150
Total	10,150

The business adopts a date of 31 December as its year end.

The car was traded in for a replacement vehicle in August 20X5 at an agreed value of $5,000.

It has been depreciated at 25 per cent per annum on the reducing-balance method, charging a full year's depreciation in the year of purchase and none in the year of sale.

What was the profit or loss on disposal of the vehicle during the year ended December 20X5?

A Profit: $718

B Profit: $781

C Profit: $1,788

D Profit: $1,836 **(2 marks)**

94 **The reducing balance method of depreciating non-current assets is more appropriate than the straight-line method when:**

A there is no expected residual value for the asset

B the expected life of the asset is not capable of being estimated

C the asset is expected to be replaced in a short period of time

D the asset decreases in value less in later years than in the early years of use **(2 marks)**

95 **SSG bought a machine for $40,000 in January 20X1. The machine had an expected useful life of six years and an expected residual value of $10,000. The machine was depreciated on the straight-line basis. At the end of December 20X4, the machine was sold for $15,000. SSG charges pro rata depreciation.**

The total amount charged to the income statement over the life of the machine was:

A $15,000

B $20,000

C $25,000

D $30,000 **(2 marks)**

96 **Liza bought a guillotine for her framing business for $20,000 on 1 July 20X7. She expected the guillotine to have a useful life of ten years and a residual value of $500.**

On 1 July 20X8, Liza revises these estimations and believes the guillotine to have a remaining useful life of 5 years and no residual value.

What is the depreciation charge for the year ended 30 June 20X9?

A $3,220

B $3,610

C $4,000

D $3,600 **(2 marks)**

FROM TRIAL BALANCE TO FINANCIAL STATEMENTS

97 **Lord has extracted the following balances from his accounts:**

	$
Plant and machinery	89,000
Property	120,000
Inventory	4,600
Payables	6,300
Receivables	5,900
Bank overdraft	790
Loan	50,000
Capital	100,000
Drawings	23,000
Sales	330,000
Purchases	165,000
Sales returns	7,000
Discounts allowed	3,200
Discounts received	?
Sundry expenses	73,890

He has forgotten to extract the balance from the discounts received account. What is the balance?

A $1,900

B $9,500

C $4,500

D $15,900 **(2 marks)**

98 Which of the following statements are true?

(1) The trial balance provides a check that no errors exist in the accounting records of a business.

(2) The trial balance is a first step in the preparation of the financial statements.

A 1 only

B 2 only

C Both 1 and 2

D Neither 1 nor 2 **(2 marks)**

99 Which of the following are limitations of the trial balance?

1 It does not include final figures to be included in the financial statements.

2 It does not identify errors of commission.

3 It does not identify in what accounts errors have been made.

A 1 and 2

B 2 and 3 only

C All 3 **(1 mark)**

100 The following is an extract from the trial balance of Gardeners:

	Dr	*Cr*
	$	$
Non-current assets	50,000	
Inventory	2,600	
Capital		28,000
Receivables	4,500	
Allowance for receivables		320
Cash	290	
Payables		5,000
Sales		120,000
Purchases	78,900	
Rental expense	3,400	
Sundry expenses	13,900	
Bank interest		270
	153,590	153,590

- Rent of $200 has been prepaid.
- Inventory at the end of the year was $1,900.
- The allowance for receivables is to be $200.

What is the profit for the year?

A $23,690

B $23,610

C $23,100

D $25,500 **(2 marks)**

101 The following is an extract from the trial balance of Ardbark, a company. After making corrections, what is the revised balance on the suspense account?

	Dr	*Cr*
	$	$
Premises	500,000	
Provision for depreciation		120,000
Inventory		23,000
Share capital	200,000	
Retained profits		105,000
Receivables	43,500	
Carriage in		1,500
Allowance for receivables		3,400
Bank overdraft	1,010	
Payables		35,900
Sales		500,080
Purchases	359,700	
Sales returns	10,300	
Sundry expenses	14,000	
Discounts allowed		1,340
Suspense		338,290
	1,128,510	1,128,510

A $15,710 Dr

B $14,730 Dr

C $12,050Dr

D $33,630 Dr **(2 marks)**

102 The following year end adjustments are required:

- Closing inventory of $45,700 to be recorded.
- Depreciation at 20% straight line to be charged on assets with a cost cf $470,800.
- An Irrecoverable debt of $230 to be written off.
- Deferred income of $6,700 to be recorded.

What is the impact on net assets of these adjustments?

A $55,390 increase

B $55,390 decrease

C $41,990 decrease

D $41,990 increase **(2 marks)**

103 The following is the extract of Jordan's trial balance as at 31 December 20X7:

	DR	*CR*
	$	$
Rent	22,000	
Insurance	30,000	

The following notes have been provided:

(i) The monthly rent charge is $2,000.

(ii) The annual insurance charge for the above year is $28,000.

What is the charge for rent and insurance for the year and the closing accrual and prepayment?

		Charge for the year		*Closing*
		$		$
A	Rent	22,000	Rent prepayment	2,000
	Insurance	28,000	Insurance prepayment	2,000
B	Rent	22,000	Rent accrual	2,000
	Insurance	30,000	Insurance prepayment	2,000
C	Rent	24,000	Rent accrual	2,000
	Insurance	28,000	Insurance prepayment	2,000
D	Rent	24,000	Rent accrual	2,000
	Insurance	30,000	Insurance accrual	2,000

(2 marks)

104 The following is the extract of Jim's trial balance as at 31 December 20X7:

	DR	*CR*
	$	$
Receivables	29,600	
Allowance for receivables		3,100
Irrecoverable debts	1,600	

The following notes are provided.

(i) Additional irrecoverable debts of $3,000 were discovered at the year end.

(ii) It has been decided to make an allowance for receivables of 10% on the adjusted receivables at the year end.

The total bad debt expense (irrecoverable debts and allowances for receivables) for the year ended 31 December 20X7 and the closing net receivables balance as at 31 December 20X7 will be:

	Bad debts expense	*Net receivables*
	$	$
A	4,160	23,940
B	5,040	23,940
C	2,560	21,830
D	4,000	19,800

(2 marks)

105 The following is the extract of Jenny's trial balance as at 31 December 20X7:

	DR	*CR*
	$	$
Plant and machinery	50,000	
Plant and machinery accumulated depreciation		15,000

The policy of the business is to charge depreciation at 10% per annum on a straight line basis.

What is the income statement depreciation charge for the year ended 31 December 20X7 and the closing net book value as at 31 December 20X7

	Depreciation charge	*Net book value*
	$	$
A	3,500	31,500
B	5,000	30,000
C	5,000	45,000
D	3,500	30,000

(2 marks)

106 The following is the extract of Julian's trial balance as at 31 December 20X7:

	DR	*CR*
	$	$
Motor vehicles	50,000	
Motor vehicles accumulated depreciation		21,875

The policy of the business is to charge depreciation at 25% per annum on a reducing balance basis.

What is the income statement depreciation charge for the year ended 31 December 20X7 and the closing net book value as at 31 December 20X7?

Calculations to be rounded to the nearest $.

	Depreciation charge	*Net book value*
	$	$
A	12,500	15,625
B	7,031	42,969
C	12,500	37,500
D	7,031	21,094

(2 marks)

BOOKS OF PRIME ENTRY AND CONTROL ACCOUNTS

107 Which of the following are books of prime entry?

A Sales day book and trial balance

B Petty cash book and accounts receivables ledger

C Petty cash book and journal

(1 mark)

108 The petty cash balance at 30 November 20X9 was $25. The following transactions occurred during the month:

1 Biscuits were purchased at a cost of $7.25.

2 Travel expenses of $12.75 were reimbursed to an employee.

3 The cleaner was paid $15.

What is the imprest amount?

A $25

B $60

C $35

D $50

(2 marks)

109 Within a petty cash system:

Balance at start of month	X
Expenses during month	(Y)
Amount transferred from bank	<u>Z</u>
Balance at end of month	<u>Q</u>

Which of the following are true?

A X = Q and Y = Z

B X = Z and Y = Q

(1 mark)

110 You are given the following figures for sales and receivables:

	20X7	*20X6*
	$	$
Receivables at year end	74,963	69,472
Sales	697,104	
Total cash received from customers	686,912	
General allowance for receivables	750	695
Specific allowance for receivables	1,264	
Irrecoverable debts written off	1,697	

What was the value of sales returns during 20X7?

A $1,740

B $2,949

C $3,004

D $4,268 **(2 marks)**

111 Ignacius operates the imprest system for petty cash. At 1 July there was a float of $150, but it was decided to increase this to $200 from 1 August onwards. During July, the petty cashier received $25 from staff for using the photocopier and a cheque for $90 was cashed for an employee. In July, cheques were drawn for $500 for petty cash.

How much cash was paid out as cash expenses by the petty cashier in July?

A $385

B $435

C $515

D $615 **(2 marks)**

112 Which ONE of the following might explain a debit balance on a payables ledger account?

A The company took a cash discount to which it was not entitled and paid less than the amount due

B The company mistakenly paid too much

C The book-keeper failed to enter a contra with the receivables ledger

D The book-keeper failed to post a cheque paid to the account **(2 marks)**

113 Allister's payables ledger control account has a balance at 1 October 20X8 of $34,500 credit.

During October, credit purchases were $78,400, cash purchases were $2,400 and payments made to suppliers, excluding cash purchases, and after deducting cash discounts of $1,200, were $68,900. Purchase returns were $4,700.

The closing balance was:

A $38,100

B $40,500

C $47,500

D $49,900 **(2 marks)**

114 The entries in a receivables ledger control account are:

Sales	$250,000
Bank	$225,000
Returns	$2,500
Irrecoverable debts	$3,000
Returned unpaid cheque	$3,500
Contra payables ledger account	$4,000

What is the balance on the receivables ledger control account?

A $12,000

B $19,000

C $25,000

D $27,000 **(2 marks)**

115 Which of the following is not the purpose of a receivables ledger control account?

A To provide a check on the arithmetic accuracy of the personal ledger

B To help to locate errors in the trial balance

C To ensure that there are no errors in the personal ledger **(1 mark)**

116 A credit entry of $450 on X's account in the books of Y could have arisen by:

A X buying goods on credit from Y

B Y paying X $450

C Y returning goods to X

D X returning goods to Y **(2 marks)**

117 Which of the following best describes the entries that are made using the sales day book totals at the end of each month?

A Debit sales with total net sales, credit receivables ledger control with total gross sales and credit sales tax account with total sales tax

B Debit sales with total gross sales, credit receivables ledger control with total net sales and credit sales tax account with total sales tax

C Debit receivables ledger control with total net sales, debit sales tax account with total sales tax and credit sales with total gross sales

D Debit receivables ledger control with total gross sales, credit sales with total net sales and credit sales tax account with total sales tax **(2 marks)**

118 A business' petty cash operates on an imprest system with an imprest of $100. All claims for payment must be supported by a third party voucher such as a receipt. Which of the following is the most cost-effective control that should be implemented in addition to the imprest?

A A designated petty cash cashier

B The petty cash tin kept in a locked drawer in a supervisor's office

C The imprest should be kept in a safe rather than a locked box

D Claims should be counter-signed by a manager **(2 marks)**

119 Which of the following best describes the purpose of a purchase invoice?

A Issued by a supplier as a request for payment

B Sent to supplier as a request for a supply

C Issued by supplier listing details of recent transactions

D Sent to the supplier as notification of payment **(2 marks)**

120 Which of the following are documents issued by the customer in a transaction rather than the supplier?

A Quotation, goods delivery note and debit note

B Goods delivery note, remittance advice and sales order

C Purchase order and debit note

D Sales order, purchase invoice and remittance advice **(2 marks)**

CONTROL ACCOUNT RECONCILIATIONS

121 A payables ledger control account showed a credit balance of $768,420. The payables ledger totalled $781,200.

Which one of the following possible errors could account in full for the difference?

A A contra against a receivables ledger debit balance of $6,390 has been entered on the credit side of the payables ledger control account

B The total of discounts allowed $28,400 was entered to the debit side of the payables ledger control account instead of the correct figure for discounts received of $15,620

C $12,780 cash paid to a supplier was entered on the credit side of the supplier's account on the payables ledger

D The total of discounts received $6,390 has been entered on the credit side of the payables ledger control account **(2 marks)**

122 The payables ledger control account below contains a number of errors:

Payables ledger control account

	$		$
Balance b/f	318,600		
Cash paid to suppliers	1,364,300	Purchases	1,268,600
Purchase returns	41,200	Contras against debit balances in receivables ledger	48,000
Refunds received from suppliers	2,700	Discounts received	8,200
		Balance c/f	402,000
	1,726,800		1,726,800

All items relate to credit purchases.

What should be the closing balance when all the errors are corrected?

A $128,200

B $509,000

C $224,200

D $144,600 **(2 marks)**

123 Ordan received a statement from one of its suppliers, Alta, showing a balance due of $3,980. the amount due according to the payables ledger account of Ordan was only $230.

Comparison of the statement and the ledger account revealed the following differences:

1 A cheque sent by Ordan for $270 has not been allowed for in Alta's statement.

2 Alta has not allowed for goods returned by Ordan $180.

3 Ordan made a contra entry, reducing the amount due to Alta by $3,200, for a balance due from Alta in Ordan's receivables ledger. No such entry has been made in Alta's records.

What difference remains between the two companies' records after adjusting for these items?

A $460

B $640

C $6,500

D $100 **(2 marks)**

124 A business' sales (receivables) ledger control account did not agree with the total of the balances on the receivables ledger. An investigation revealed that the sales day book had been overcast by $10. What effect will this have on the discrepancy?

A The control account should be credited with $10

B The control account should be debited with $10 **(1 mark)**

125 A supplier sends Lord a statement showing a balance outstanding of $14,350. Lord's records show a balance outstanding of $14,500.

The reason for this difference could be that:

A the supplier sent an invoice for $150 which you have not yet received

B the supplier has allowed you $150 cash discount which you had omitted to enter in your ledgers

C you have paid the supplier $150 which he has not yet accounted for

D you have returned goods worth $150 which the supplier has not yet accounted for **(2 marks)**

126 Which of the following would NOT lead to a difference between the total of the balances on the receivables ledger and the balance on the receivables ledger control account?

A An error in totalling the sales day book

B An error in totalling the receipts column of the cash book

C An overstatement of an entry in a customer's account

D An entry posted to the wrong customer's account **(2 marks)**

127 A receivables ledger control account showed a debit balance of $37,642. The individual customers' accounts in the receivables ledger showed a total of $35,840. The difference could be due to:

A undercasting the sales day book by $1,802

B overcasting the sales returns day book by $1,802

C entering a cash receipt of $1,802 on the debit side of a customer's account

D entering a cash discount allowed of $901 on the debit side of the control account **(2 marks)**

128 Tarbuck has received a statement of account from one of its suppliers, showing an outstanding balance due to them of $1,350. On comparison with the ledger account, the following is determined:

- The ledger account shows a credit balance of $260.
- The supplier has disallowed a cash discount of $80 due to late payment of an invoice.
- The supplier has not yet allowed for goods returned at the end of the period of $270.
- Cash in transit of $830 has not been received by the supplier.

Following consideration of these items, the unreconciled difference between the two records is:

A $70

B $90

C $430

D $590 **(2 marks)**

129 The purchase day book of Arbroath has been undercast by $500, and the sales day book has been overcast by $700. Arbroath maintains payables and receivables ledger control accounts as part of the double entry bookkeeping system.

The effect of correcting these errors will be to:

A make adjustments to the ledger balances of the individual customers and suppliers, with no effect on profit

B make adjustments to the ledger balances of the individual customers and suppliers, with a decrease in profit of $1,200

C make adjustments to the control accounts, with no effect on profit

D make adjustments to the control accounts, with a decrease in profit of $1,200 **(2 marks)**

130 For the month of November 20X0 Figgin's purchases totalled $225,600 with sales tax of $33,840. The total of $259,440 has been credited to the payables ledger control account as $254,940.

Which of the following adjustments is correct?

	Control account	*List of suppliers' balances*
A	$4,500 Cr	No adjustment
B	$4,500 Cr	Increase by $4,500
C	$29,340 Dr	No effect
D	$33,840 Dr	Increase by $4,500

(2 marks)

131 In reconciling the receivables ledger control account with the list of receivables ledger balances of SK, the following errors were found:

1 The sales day book had been overcast by $370.

2 A total of $940 from the cash receipts book had been recorded in the receivables ledger control account as $490.

What adjustments must be made to correct the errors?

A Credit sales control account $820. Decrease total of receivables ledger balances by $820

B Credit sales control account $820. No change in total of receivables ledger balances.

C Debit sales control account $80. No change in total of receivables ledger balances

D Debit sales control account $80. Increase total of receivables ledger balances by $80

(2 marks)

BANK RECONCILIATIONS

132 The cash book of Worcester shows a credit balance of $1,350. Cheques of $56 have been written to suppliers but not yet cleared the bank; uncleared lodgements amount to $128. The bank has accidentally credited Worcester's account with interest of $15 due to another customer. A standing order of $300 has not been accounted for in the general ledger. What is the balance on the bank statement?

A $993 Cr

B $993 Dr

C $1,707 Cr

D $1,707 Dr **(2 marks)**

133 Jo's bank ledger account shows a balance of $190 credit. Her bank statement reports a balance of $250 credit.

Which of the following will explain the difference in full?

A Unpresented cheques of $100 and an uncleared lodgement of $30

B Unpresented cheques of $150, the misposting of a cash receipt of $130 to the wrong side of the cash account and unrecorded bank interest received of $30

C An unrecorded direct debit of $30, a dishonoured cheque of $70 and an uncleared lodgement of $40

D An unrecorded standing order of $60, an unpresented cheque of $110 and a bank error whereby Jo's account was accidentally credited with $110 **(2 marks)**

134 Which of the following statements about bank reconciliations are correct?

(1) In preparing a bank reconciliation, unpresented cheques must be deducted from a balance of cash at bank shown in the bank statement.

(2) A cheque from a customer paid into the bank but dishonoured must be corrected by making a debit entry in the cash book.

(3) An error by the bank must be corrected by an entry in the cash book.

(4) An overdraft is a debit balance in the bank statement.

A 1 and 3

B 2 and 3

C 1 and 4

D 2 and 4 **(2 marks)**

135 The following bank reconciliation statement has been prepared by an inexperienced bookkeeper at 31 December 20X5:

	$
Balance per bank statement (overdrawn)	38,640
Add: Lodgments not credited	19,270
	57,910
Less: Unpresented cheques	14,260
Balance per cash book	43,650

What should the final cash book balance be when all the above items have been properly dealt with?

A $43,650 overdrawn

B $33,630 overdrawn

C $5,110 overdrawn

D $72,170 overdrawn **(2 marks)**

136 A bank reconciliation statement for Dallas at 30 June 20X5 is being prepared. The following information is available:

1 Bank charges of $2,340 have not been entered in the cash book.

2 The bank statement shows a balance of $200 Dr.

3 Unpresented cheques amount to $1,250.

4 A direct debit of $250 has not been recorded in the ledger accounts.

5 A bank error has resulted in a cheque for $97 being debited to Dallas' account instead of Dynasty's account.

6 Cheques received but not yet banked amounted to $890.

The final balance in the cash book after all necessary adjustments should be

A $463 Dr

B $463 Cr

C $63 Cr

D $63 Dr **(2 marks)**

137 The following information relates to a bank reconciliation.

1 The bank balance in the cash book before taking the items below into account was $8,970 overdrawn.

2 Bank charges of $550 on the bank statement have not been entered in the cash book.

3 The bank has credited the account in error with $425 which belongs to another customer.

4 Cheque payments totalling $3,275 have been entered in the cashbook but have not been presented for payment.

5 Cheques totalling $5,380 have been correctly entered on the debit side of the cashbook but have not been paid in at the bank.

What was the balance as shown by the bank statement before taking the items above into account?

A $8,970 overdrawn

B $11,200 overdrawn

C $12,050 overdrawn

D $17,750 overdrawn **(2 marks)**

138 Sharmin's bank statement at 31 October 20X8 shows a balance of $13,400. She subsequently discovers that the bank has dishonoured a customer's cheque for $300 and has charged bank charges of $50, neither of which is recorded in the cash book.

There are unpresented cheques totalling $1,400and an automatic receipt from a customer of $195 has been recorded as a credit in Sharmin's cash book.

Sharmin's cash book balance, prior to correcting the errors and omissions, was:

A $11,455

B $11,960

C $12,000

D $12,155 **(2 marks)**

139 Wimborne's bank statement shows a balance of $715 overdrawn. The statement includes bank charges of $74 which have not been entered in the cash book. There are also unpresented cheques totalling $824 and lodgements not yet credited of $337. In addition the bank statement erroneously includes a dividend receipt of $25 belonging to another customer.

The bank overdraft in the statement of financial position should be:

A $253

B $1,177

C $1,202

D $1,227 **(2 marks)**

140 The cash book shows a bank balance of $5,675 overdrawn at 31 August 20X5. It is subsequently discovered that a standing order for $125 has been entered twice, and that a dishonoured cheque for $450 has been debited in the cash book instead of credited. The correct bank balance should be:

A $5,100 overdrawn

B $6,000 overdrawn

C $6,250 overdrawn

D $6,450 overdrawn **(2 marks)**

141 An organisation's cash book has an opening balance of $485 credit. The following transactions then took place:

Cash sales $1,450 including sales tax of $150.

Receipts from customers of debts of $2,400.

Payments to suppliers of debts of $1,800 less 5% cash discount.

Dishonoured cheques from customers amounting to $250.

The resulting balance in the cash book should be:

A $1,255 debit

B $1,405 debit

C $1,905 credit

D $2,375 credit **(2 marks)**

142 The bank statement at 31 October 20X7 showed an overdraft of $800. On reconciling the bank statement, it was discovered that a cheque drawn by your company for $80 had not been presented for payment, and that a cheque for $130 from a customer had been dishonoured on 30 October 20X7, but that this had not yet been notified to you by the bank.

The correct bank balance to be shown in the statement of financial position at 31 October 20X7 is:

A $1,010 overdrawn

B $880 overdrawn

C $750 overdrawn

D $720 overdrawn **(2 marks)**

143 Your firm's cash book at 30 April 20X8 shows a balance at the bank of $2,490. Comparison with the bank statement at the same date reveals the following differences:

	$
Unpresented cheques	840
Bank charges not in cash book	50
Receipts not yet credited by the bank	470
Dishonoured cheque not in cash book	140

The correct bank balance at 30 April 20X8 is:

A $1,460

B $2,300

C $2,580

D $3,140 **(2 marks)**

144 Your firm's cash book shows a credit bank balance of $1,240 at 30 April 20X9. On comparison with the bank statement, you determine that there are unpresented cheques totalling $450, and a receipt of $140 which has not yet been passed through the bank account. The bank statement shows bank charges of $75 which have not been entered in the cash book.

The balance on the bank statement is:

A $1,005 overdrawn

B $930 overdrawn

C $1,475 in credit

D $1,550 in credit **(2 marks)**

145 Which of the following is not an 'unrecorded difference' when reconciling the balance on the cash book to the amount shown in the bank statement?

A A standing order

B Bank interest

C An uncleared lodgement **(1 mark)**

CORRECTION OF ERRORS AND SUSPENSE ACCOUNTS

146 A trial balance shows a total of debits of $347,800 and a total of credits of $362,350.

After adjusting for the following errors, what is the balance on the suspense account?

(1) A credit sale of $3,670 was incorrectly entered in the sales day book as $3,760.

(2) A non-current asset with a carrying value of $7,890 was disposed of for $9,000. The only accounting entry was to debit cash.

(3) The allowance for receivables was increased from $8,900 to $10,200. The allowance account was debited in error.

A $26,150 debit

B $26,060 debit

C $26,240 debit

D $2,950 credit **(2 marks)**

147 The trial balance of Kelvin does not balance. Which two of the following errors could explain this, assuming that Kelvin maintains control accounts for its receivables and payables within the double entry system?

(1) The sales day book was undercast by $100.

(2) Discounts allowed were debited to the discounts received account.

(3) An opening accrual was omitted from the rent account.

(4) The debit side of the cash account was undercast.

A 1 and 2

B 2 and 3

C 3 and 4

D 1 and 4 **(2 marks)**

148 The trial balance of MHSB does not balance at the year end. What type of error may explain this?

A Extraction error

B Error of commission

C Compensating error **(1 mark)**

149 The trial balance of Bob Butler shows total debits of $125,819 and total credits of $118,251. Which of the following explains the difference in full?

A Discounts allowed of $3,784 have been shown on the wrong side of the trial balance.

B Discounts received of $3,784 have been credited to the payables ledger control account.

C The sales day book has been undercast by $7,568.

D An opening accrual of $7,568 has been omitted from the rental expense account.

(2 marks)

150 Which one of the following journals is correct according to its narrative?

		Debit $	Credit $
A	Mr Smith personal account	100,000	
	Directors' remuneration		100,000
	Bonus allocated to account of managing director (Mr Smith)		
B	Purchases	14,000	
	Wages	24,000	
	Repairs to buildings		38,000
	Transfer of costs of repairs to buildings carried out by company employees using materials from inventory		
C	Discounts allowed	2,800	
	Discounts received		2,800
	Correction of error: discounts allowed total incorrectly debited to discounts received account.		
D	Suspense account	20,000	
	Rent receivable		10,000
	Rent payable		10,000
	Correction of error: rent received credited in error to rent payable account.		

(2 marks)

151 The trial balance of Koi did not balance, and a suspense account was opened for the difference.

Which of the following errors would require an entry to the suspense account in correcting them?

1 A cash payment to purchase a motor van had been correctly entered in the cash book but had been debited to the motor expenses account.

2 The debit side of the wages account had been undercast.

3 The total of the discounts allowed column in the cash book had been posted to the receivables ledger control account correctly and credited to the discounts received account.

4 A cash refund to a customer had been recorded by debiting the cash book and crediting the customer's account.

A 1 and 2

B 2 and 3

C 3 and 4

D 2 and 4 **(2 marks)**

152 A company's trial balance failed to agree, and a suspense account was opened for the difference.

Subsequent checking revealed that discounts allowed of $13,000 had been credited to the discounts received account and an entry on the credit side of the cash book for the purchase of some machinery costing $18,000 had not been posted to the plant and machinery account.

Which two of the following journal entries would correct the errors?

		Debit	*Credit*
		$	$
1	Discounts allowed	13,000	
	Discounts received		13,000
2	Discounts allowed	13,000	
	Discounts received	13,000	
	Suspense account		26,000
3	Suspense account	26,000	
	Discounts allowed		13,000
	Discounts received		13,000
4	Plant and machinery	18,000	
	Suspense account		18,000
5	Suspense account	18,000	
	Plant and machinery		18,000

A 1 and 4

B 2 and 5

C 2 and 4

D 3 and 5 **(2 marks)**

This information is relevant to the following TWO questions:

A company's draft financial statements for 20X5 showed a profit of $630,000. However, the trial balance did not agree, and a suspense account appeared in the company's financial statements.

Subsequent checking revealed the following errors:

1 The cost of an item of plant $48,000 had been entered in the cash book and in the plant account as $4,800.Depreciation at the rate of 10% per year ($480) had been charged.

2 Bank charges of $440 appeared in the bank statement in December 20X5 but had not been entered in the company's records.

3 One of the directors paid $800 due to a supplier in the company's payables ledger by a personal cheque. The bookkeeper recorded a debit in the supplier's ledger account but did not complete the double entry for the transaction (The company does not maintain a payables ledger control account).

4 The payments side of the cash book had been understated by $10,000.

153 Which of the above items would require an entry to the suspense account in correcting them?

A All four items

B 3 and 4 only

C 2 and 3 only

D 1, 2 and 4 only **(2 marks)**

154 What would the company's profit become after the correction of the above errors?

A $634,760

B $624,760

C $624,440

D $625,240 **(2 marks)**

155 The draft accounts of Galahad's business for the year ended 31 July 20X0 show a profit of $54,250 prior to the correction of the following errors:

1 Cash drawings of $250 have not been accounted for.

2 Debts amounting to $420, which were provided against in full during the year, should have been written off as irrecoverable.

3 Rental income of $300 has been classified as interest receivable.

4 On the last day of the accounting period, $200 in cash was received from a customer, but no bookkeeping entries have yet been made.

What is the correct profit of the business for the year?

A $53,580

B $53,830

C $54,250

D $55,830 **(2 marks)**

156 The trial balance of Flo, a limited liability company, does not agree and a suspense account has been opened.

Inventory bought at a tax inclusive cost of $4,700 has been credited to the payables ledger control account. The sales tax, at 17.5%, has been recorded in the sales tax account and the total $4,700 has been recorded in the purchases account.

What entry is required to correct the error?

A	Dr Payables ledger control account $700	Cr Suspense account $700
B	Dr Payables ledger control account $822.50	Cr Suspense account $822.50
C	Dr Suspense account $700	Cr Purchases $700
D	Dr Suspense account $822.50	Cr Purchases $822.50

(2 marks)

157 Weagan's trial balance at 31 October 20X9 is out of agreement, with the debit side totalling $500 less than the credit side. During November, the following errors are discovered:

- The credit side of the sales account for October had been undercast by $150.
- Rent received of $240 had been credited to the rent payable account.
- The allowance for receivables, which decreased by $420, had been recorded in the allowance for receivables account as an increase.

Following the correction of these errors, the balance on the suspense account would be:

A $190 Cr

B $670 Cr

C $1,190 Cr

D $1,490 Dr **(2 marks)**

158 Which ONE of the following is an error of principle?

A A gas bill credited to the gas account and debited to the bank account

B The purchase of a non-current asset credited to the asset at cost account and debited to the supplier's account

C The purchase of a non-current asset debited to the purchases account and credited to the supplier's account

D The payment of wages debited and credited to the correct accounts, but using the wrong amount **(2 marks)**

159 The trial balance of C did not agree, and a suspense account was opened for the difference. Checking in the bookkeeping system revealed a number of errors:

Error

1 $4,600 paid for motor van repairs was correctly treated in the cash book but was credited to motor vehicles asset account.

2 $360 received from Brown, a customer, was credited in error to the account of Green.

3 $9,500 paid for rent was debited to the rent account as $5,900.

4 The total of the discount allowed column in the cash book had been debited in error to the discounts received account.

5 No entries had been made to record a cash sale of $100.

Which of the errors above would require an entry to the suspense account as part of the process of correcting them?

A Errors 3 and 4 only

B Errors 1 and 3 only

C Errors 2 and 5 only

D Errors 2 and 3 only **(2 marks)**

160 Drive gives a cash discount of $40 to a customer. The discount is credited to the discounts allowed account.

The effect of recording the discount in this way is that profit will be:

A correct

B overstated by $80

C understated by $80

D understated by $40. **(2 marks)**

161 A suspense account was opened when a trial balance failed to agree. The following errors were later discovered:

Error

1 A gas bill of $420 had been recorded in the Gas account as $240.

2 Discount of $50 given to a customer had been credited to Discounts Received.

3 Interest received of $70 had been entered in the bank account only.

The original balance on the suspense account was:

A debit $210

B credit $210

C debit $160

D credit $160 **(2 marks)**

162 The book-keeper of High Hurdles was instructed to make a contra entry for $270 between the supplier account and the customer account for Greyfold. He recorded the transaction by debiting the customer account and crediting the supplier account with $270. The business accounts do not include control accounts.

Which of the following statements is correct?

A Unless the error is corrected, profit will be over-stated by $540

B Unless the error is corrected, net assets will be over-stated by $270

C Unless the error is corrected, net assets will be over-stated by $540

D The errors should be corrected, but neither the profit nor the net assets are over-stated

(2 marks)

APPLICATIONS OF INFORMATION TECHNOLOGY

163 Which of the following are advantages of computerised accounting systems?

1 A computer runs under the control of a stored program meaning that only limited operator activity is required.

2 Computer systems are flexible and can be altered quickly and at little cost.

3 Computers can recognise and highlight errors and incomplete or incorrect data.

4 The computer can be programmed to undertake complicated decision making processes.

A 1 and 2

B All 4

C 1 and 4

D 2 and 3 **(2 marks)**

164 Which of the following is NOT an advantage of a database over a manual card index system?

A May be used to generate reports

B Can hold more information

C Calculations can be performed automatically

D Records matching a certain criterion can be selected **(2 marks)**

165 Which of the following statements is true?

1 In a computerised system, all accounting personnel will have access to all records.

2 The general ledger in a computerised system tends to take the same format as that in a manual system, i.e. a number of T accounts.

A Neither 1 nor 2

B Both 1 and 2

C 1 only

D 2 only **(2 marks)**

166 Which of the following best describes an integrated accounting package?

A A computerised package which has grown piecemeal, with the most detailed areas of accounting being computerised first

B A computerised package which handles all parts of the accounting process and produces the financial statements

C A computerised package that can be used for 'modelling' type applications such as forecasting

D A computerised package that includes word processing, spreadsheets and database systems **(2 marks)**

167 Which of the following is / are features of a spreadsheet?

1 Goal-seeking facility.

2 Flexibility.

3 Look up tables.

4 'What if' analysis.

5 Graphics.

A All 5

B 1, 2, 3 and 4

C 1, 2 and 4

D 3 and 5 **(2 marks)**

INCOMPLETE RECORDS

168 On 1 September 20X8, Winston had inventory of $380,000. During the month, sales totalled $650,000 and purchases $480,000. On 30 September 20X8 a fire destroyed some of the inventory. The undamaged goods were valued at $220,000. The business operates with a standard gross profit margin of 30%.

Based on this information, what is the cost of the inventory destroyed in the fire?

A $185,000

B $140,000

C $405,000

D $360,000 **(2 marks)**

169 The following information is available about the transactions of Razil, a sole trader who does not keep proper accounting records:

	$
Opening inventory	77,000
Closing inventory	84,000
Purchases	763,000
Gross profit margin	30%

Based on this information, what is Razil's sales revenue for the year?

A $982,800

B $1,090,000

C $2,520,000

D $1,080,000 **(2 marks)**

170 You are given the following incomplete and incorrect extract from the income statement of a company that trades at a mark up of 25% on cost:

	$	$
Sales		174,258
Less: Cost of goods sold		
Opening inventory	12,274	
Purchases	136,527	
Closing inventory	X	
		(X)
Gross profit		X

Having discovered that the sales figure should have been $174,825 and that purchase returns of $1,084 and sales returns of $1,146 have been omitted, the closing inventory should be:

A $8,662

B $8,774

C $17,349

D $17,458 **(2 marks)**

171 A fire in the offices of Lewis has destroyed most of the accounting records.

The following information has been retrieved:

	$
Sales	630,000
Opening inventory	24,300
Closing inventory	32,750
Opening payables	29,780
Closing payables	34,600

Gross profit for the period should represent a mark up of 40%.

What was the total cash paid to suppliers in the year?

A $463,270

B $381,630

C $391,270

D $453,630 **(2 marks)**

172 Pioneer's annual inventory count took place on 6 January 20X6. The value of inventory on this date was $32,780. During the period from 31 December 20X5 to 6 January 20X6, the following events occurred:

Sales	$8,600
Purchases	$4,200

The value of inventory at 31 December 20X5 was $34,600.

What is the gross margin of Pioneer?

A 70%

B 72%

C 30%

D 43% **(2 marks)**

173 Harry has a mark up of 25% on cost of sales. The following information is also available:

	$
Receivables at start of year	6,340
Receivables at end of year	5,200
Cash at start of year	620
Cash at end of year	500
Total cash payments	16,780

The only receipts during the year consisted of cash and cheques received from customers.

What is the gross profit for the year?

A $3,880

B $3,152

C $3,560

D $3,104 **(2 marks)**

174 During September, Edel had sales of $148,000, which made a gross profit of $40,000. Purchases amounted to $100,000 and opening inventory was $34,000.

The value of closing inventory was:

A $24,000

B $26,000

C $42,000

D $54,000 **(2 marks)**

175 The gross profit mark-up is 40% where:

A sales are $120,000 and gross profit is $48,000

B sales are $120,000 and cost of sales is $72,000

C sales are $100,800 and cost of sales is $72,000

D sales are $100,800 and cost of sales is $60,480 **(2 marks)**

176 From the following information, calculate the value of purchases:

	$
Opening trade payables	142,600
Cash paid	542,300
Discounts received	13,200
Goods returned	27,500
Closing trade payables	137,800

A $302,600

B $506,400

C $523,200

D $578,200 **(2 marks)**

177 You are given the following information:

Receivables at 1 January 20X3	$10,000
Receivables at 31 December 20X3	$9,000
Total receipts during 20X3 (including cash sales of $5,000)	$85,000

Sales during 20X3 amount to:

A $81,000

B $86,000

C $79,000

D $84,000 **(2 marks)**

178 P is a sole proprietor whose accounting records are incomplete. All the sales are cash sales and during the year $50,000 was banked, including $5,000 from the sale of a business car. He paid $12,000 wages in cash from the till and withdrew $2,000 per month as drawings. The cash in the till at the beginning and end of the year was $300 and $400 respectively.

What were the sales for the year?

A $80,900

B $81,000

C $81,100

D $86,100 **(2 marks)**

179 Many of the records of G have been destroyed by fire. The following information is available for the period under review.

(i) Sales totalled $480,000.

(ii) Inventory at cost was opening $36,420, closing $40,680.

(iii) Trade payables were opening $29,590, closing $33,875.

(iv) Gross profit for the period should represent a mark-up on cost of 50%.

What was the total for the period of cash paid to suppliers?

A $239,975

B $315,715

C $319,975

D $328,545 **(2 marks)**

180 Pike runs an angling shop in the south of Spain. He spends all of his spare time fishing and consequently has kept no accounting records in the year ended 31 August 20X5. He knows that he has taken $6,800 cash out of his business during the year plus bait which cost the business $250. He can also remember putting his $20,000 winnings on the Spanish lottery into the business in March.

Pike knows that at the last year end his business had assets of $40,000 and liabilities of $14,600. He has also calculated that the assets of the business at 31 August 20X5 are worth $56,000, and the liabilities $18,750.

What profit or loss has Pike made in the year?

A $1,100 profit

B $1,100 loss

C $1,350 profit

D $1,350 loss **(2 marks)**

181 Ives makes and sells hand made pottery. He keeps all finished items in a storeroom at the back of his workshop on the banks of the River Flow. In August 20X5, freak weather conditions led to extensive flooding, and Ives lost pottery which had cost $3,400 and had a retail value of $5,750.

Ives was insured for loss of inventory due to flooding.

What double entry is required to record the loss of inventory?

	Dr	*Cr*
A	Expense (IS) $5,750	Cost of sales (IS) $5,750
B	Current asset (B/S) $5,750	Cost of sales (IS) $5,750
C	Expense (IS) $3,400	Cost of sales (IS) $3,400
D	Current asset (B/S) $3,400	Cost of sales (IS) $3,400

(2 marks)

PARTNERSHIP ACCOUNTS

182 Karen and Jamie are in partnership running a training consultancy. In the year ended 30 September 20X6, the business made a profit of $180,000. The partnership agreement states that Karen is to receive a salary of $25,000 and the remaining profit is shared in the ratio 3:5. During the year, Karen took $20,000 in drawings and Jamie $60,000. What amount should be credited to Karen's current account for the year?

A $20,000

B $58,125

C $63,125

D $83,125 **(2 marks)**

183 George, Freddie and Julian are in partnership running an adventure holidays business. During the year ended 30 September 20X6, the business made a profit of $250,000. The partnership agreement states that partners receive 5% interest on their capital balance at the start of the year and then share the profits in the ratio 1:2:3.

Other information relating to the partnership is as follows:

	George	*Freddie*	*Julian*
	$	$	$
Capital b/f	100,000	110,000	95,000
Current account b/f	15,600 Cr	31,200 Cr	13,000 Dr
Cash withdrawn from business	12,800	25,000	34,000

On 31 January 20X6, Julian paid an income tax bill of $12,400 from the business bank account.

What is the balance on Julian's current account at the year end?

A $62,725 Cr

B $75,125 Cr

C $88,725 Cr

D $101,125 Cr **(2 marks)**

184 What is the correct treatment of interest charged on partners' drawings in preparing a partnership's financial statements?

A Credited as income in the income statement

B Debited as an expense in the income statement

C Added to total profit in calculating partners' profit shares **(1 mark)**

185 **Jeremy and Nicky are in partnership. They share profits equally after charging a salary of $40,000 per year for Jeremy and interest on capital at 5% per year.**

At 1 January 20X6 their capital balances were:

Jeremy	$200,000
Nicky	$100,000

On 1 July 20X6, Nicky introduced a further $100,000 capital and Jeremy's salary was discontinued.

The partnership profit for the year ended 31 December 20X6 was $337,500.

What was Jeremy's total profit share for the year ended 31 December 20X6?

A $182,500

B $178,750

C $180,000

D $190,000 **(2 marks)**

186 **Albus and Brio are in partnership, sharing profits in the ratio 3:2 and preparing their accounts to 30 June each year. On 1 January 20X6, Corbin joined the partnership and the profit sharing ratio became 4:3:3 (A:B:C).**

Profits for the year ended 30 June 20X6 were:

	$
Six months ended 31.12.X5	300,000
Six months ended 30.6.X6	450,000

An irrecoverable debt of $50,000 was written off in the six months ended 30 June X6 in computing the $450,000 profit. It was agreed that this should be borne by Albus and Brio only, in their original profit sharing ratios.

What is Albus's total profit share for the year ended 30 June 20X6?

A $330,000

B $310,000

C $340,000

D $350,000 **(2 marks)**

187 **Which of the following is NOT true of a partnership?**

A Partners have joint and several liability

B Partners have unlimited liability

C Each partner is liable only for those losses which arise from contracts negotiated by themselves

D Partners are not protected from the creditors of a business **(2 marks)**

188 Which of the following are usually covered by a partnership agreement?

1 Arrangements for dissolution of partnership.

2 How profit is to be shared amongst partners.

3 Preparation and audit of accounts.

4 List of approved suppliers.

A All 4

B 1, 2 and 3

C 1 and 2

D 2 only **(2 marks)**

189 Lewis and Hamilton are in partnership, trading as 'Grease lightning mechanics'. They have made a profit of $14,750 in the year ended 31 May 20X5.

The partnership agreement provides for a salary of $12,000 to Lewis and interest on capital at 3%. Remaining profits are shared in the ratio 1:4. At the start of the year, Lewis had invested $10,000 in the business and Hamilton $20,000.

What share of profit does Hamilton receive?

A $370

B $1,480

C $2,080

D $12,670 **(2 marks)**

190 Woody and Buzz are in partnership running a toyshop. They have not had a successful year and have reported a loss of $56,000 in the year ended 30 September 20X8.

Their partnership agreement states the following:

- A salary of $9,000 for Woody and $12,000 for Buzz.
- Interest on drawings above $10,000 in the year at 5%.
- Interest on capital at 10%.
- The balance of the profits to be shared equally.

Woody has invested $30,000 in the business and Buzz $15,000. Woody took $14,000 drawings on 1 July 20X8 and Buzz took $8,000 on 1 April 20X8.

What is Woody's share of the loss?

A $28,738 loss

B $28,800 loss

C $28,825 loss

D $28,775 loss **(2 marks)**

191 Pat and Ajay and Meera are in partnership. The terms of their agreement are as follows:

- Interest on capital at 4%.
- Ajay to receive a salary of $16,000.
- Profit share 5:3:2.
- Guaranteed minimum profit share of $6,000 for Meera.

At the start of the year, capital balances were as follows:

Pat	$14,000
Ajay	$10,000
Meera	$8,000

On 1 September 20X4, Ajay put an extra $5,000 into the business.

In the year ended 28 February 20X5, the business made a profit of $42,000

What amount should be credited to Ajay's current account for the year in respect of profits?

A $23,886

B $23,508

C $23,602.50

D $23,817.96 **(2 marks)**

192 Fleurie, Beaune and Argento are in partnership as wine merchants. The details of their partnership agreement are as follows:

- Fleurie and Beaune are entitled to a salary of $15,000.
- Interest on capital is paid at 6%.
- Remaining profits are shared in the ratio 3:2:4.

Beaune has also made a loan to the business of $20,000 on 1 July 20X8. This attracts interest at a rate of 8%. Any accrued loan interest is to be adjusted through the current account.

At 1 October 20X7, balances stood at:

	Current	*Capital*
Fleurie	$23,000 Cr	$18,000
Beaune	$10,000 Dr	$20,000
Argento	$12,000 Dr	$30,000

For the year ended 30 September 20X8, the business made a profit of $76,393 (before loan interest).

What is the balance on Beaune's current account at the end of the year?

A $35,114 Cr

B $15,914 Cr

C $15,114 Cr

D $35,914 Cr **(2 marks)**

193 Orla, Anya and Chloe run a ladies' accessories shop. They have been in partnership for many years, splitting profits in the ratio 3:2:5. They decide to admit Lulu as a partner on 1 January 20X6, at which date goodwill is valued at $30,000. After the admission of Lulu, profits will be split 4:3:6:2.

On 1 January 20X6 (prior to accounting for the admission), capital and current account balances were as follows:

	Capital	*Current*
	$	$
Orla	50,000	24,300
Anya	40,000	13,250
Chloe	70,000	20,500

After accounting for the admission without using a goodwill account, what is the balance on Orla's capital and current accounts?

	Capital	*Current*
	$	$
A	50,000	23,300
B	50,000	25,300
C	51,000	24,300
D	49,000	24,300

(2 marks)

194 Macy, Bloomingdale and Saks have been in partnership for several years, sharing profits in the ratio 2:1:4. Macy would now like to take a step back from the business and to reflect her lesser involvement, and Bloomingdale's greater involvement, the profit sharing ratio is to be changed to 1:3:5.

The value of the goodwill is $63,000.

What is the impact of the transaction on Bloomingdale's total capital (current and capital accounts) balance as a result of the transaction if no goodwill account is maintained?

A $12,000 debit

B $12,000 credit

C $9,000 credit

D $9,000 debit **(2 marks)**

195 Odd and Job are in partnership and share profits in the ratio 2:3. On 1 June 20X7, a new partner, Mann joins the business, introducing $12,000 capital.

The following also take place on this date:

- Goodwill is valued at $40,000.
- The profit share ratio is revised to 3:6:1.
- Property is revalued upwards by $35,000.

If Odd's capital account had a balance of $45,000 credit prior to adjusting the accounts, what is the balance after adjustment, assuming that a goodwill account is used?

A $61,000 Cr

B $63,000 Cr

C $75,000 Cr

D $49,000 Cr **(2 marks)**

196 Which of the following are true?

1 When there is a change in the structure of a partnership, the assets of the business are normally revalued.

2 Partnership goodwill can be calculated as a multiple of the previous year's profit.

3 Partnership goodwill is only considered when a new partner joins or an old partner leaves the partnership.

A 1 and 2

B 1 and 3

C 2 and 3

D All 3 **(2 marks)**

197 Ami, Kami and Shati have been in partnership for several years. Their total profit share at the end of the year has been established as follows:

	$
Ami	18,000
Kami	20,000
Shati	25,000

Their profit share for the year is 1:2:3.

Ami is guaranteed a minimum profit share of $21,000.

What is the profit share for all the partners after adjusting for the guaranteed minimum share?

	Ami	*Kami*	*Shati*
	$	$	$
A	21,000	19,000	26,500
B	21,000	18,800	23,200
C	21,000	20,000	25,000
D	21,000	21,200	26,800

(2 marks)

COMPANY ACCOUNTS

198 The following information is relevant to Wimbledon:

	$
Opening inventory	12,500
Closing inventory	17,900
Purchases	199,000
Distribution costs	35,600
Administrative expenses	78,800
Audit fee	15,200
Carriage in	3,500
Carriage out	7,700
Depreciation	40,000

Depreciation is to be split in the ratio 30:70 between the office and factory.

What is the cost of sales?

A $233,600

B $221,600

C $225,100

D $237,100 **(2 marks)**

199 Brown has $100,000 50c shares and $400,000 8% irredeemable preference shares in issue. A dividend of 3c per ordinary share and half of the preference dividend were paid during the year.

Which of the following statements are true?

1 An ordinary dividend of $3,000 is paid during the year.

2 A preference dividend of $16,000 is accrued at the year end.

A 1 only

B 2 only

C Neither 1 nor 2

D Both 1 and 2 **(2 marks)**

200 At 1 October 20X6, Ozber's capital was structured as follows:

	$
Ordinary shares of 25c	100,000
Share premium	30,000

On 10 January 20X7, in order to raise finance for expansion, there was a 1 for 4 rights issue at $1.15. The issue was fully taken up. This was followed by a 1 for 10 bonus issue on 1 June 20X7.

What is the balance on the share premium account after these transactions?

A $17,500

B $21,250

C $107,500

D $120,000 **(2 marks)**

201 Where in a company's financial statements complying with International accounting standards, should you find dividends paid?

1 Statement of comprehensive income.

2 Statement of financial position.

3 Statement of cash flows.

4 Statement of changes in equity.

A 1 and 3

B 2 and 3

C 1 and 4

D 3 and 4 **(2 marks)**

202 Where in the financial statements should tax on profit for the current period, and unrealised surplus on revaluation of properties, be separately disclosed?

	Tax on profit for the current period	*Unrealised surplus on revaluation of properties*
A	Statement of comprehensive income	Statement of cash flows
B	Statement of changes in equity	Statement of comprehensive income
C	Statement of comprehensive income	Statement of comprehensive income

(1 mark)

203 The following information is available about a company's dividends:

Sept 20X5	Final dividend for the year ended 30 June 20X5 paid (declared August 20X5)	$100,000
March 20X6	Interim dividend for the year ended 30 June 20X6 paid	$40,000
Sept 20X6	Final dividend for the year ended 30 June 20X6 paid (declared August 20X6)	$120,000

What figures, if any, should be disclosed in the company's statement of comprehensive income for the year ended 30 June 20X6 and its statement of financial position at that date?

	Statement of comprehensive income	*Statement of financial position*
A	$160,000 deduction	$120,000
B	$140,000 deduction	Nil
C	Nil	$120,000
D	Nil	Nil

(2 marks)

204 Which of the following statements are correct?

1 A company might make a rights issue if it wished to raise more equity capital.

2 A rights issue might increase the share premium account whereas a bonus issue is likely to reduce it.

3 A rights issue will always increase the number of shareholders in a company whereas a bonus issue will not.

4 A bonus issue will result in the market value of each share increasing

A 1 and 2

B 1 and 3

C 2 and 3

D 2 and 4 **(2 marks)**

205 Florabundi, a limited liability company, shows an overprovision of $3,400 on its tax liability account at the end of the year ended 31 December 20X8 before accounting for that year's tax charge.

It estimates tax on profits for the year to be $67,900.

What amounts should be shown in the financial statements for the year ended 31 December 20X8 in respect of tax?

	Statement of comprehensive income	*Statement of financial position*
A	$67,900 tax charge	$67,900 tax payable
B	$64,500 tax charge	$64,500 tax payable
C	$64,500 tax charge	$67,900 tax payable
D	$71,300 tax charge	$67,900 tax payable

(2 marks)

206 Classify the following assets and liabilities as current or non-current in Albatross, a limited liability company's accounts:

1 A sale has been made on credit to a customer. They have agreed to terms stating that payment is due in 12 months time.

2 A bank overdraft facility of $30,000 is available under an agreement with the bank which extends 2 years.

3 A company has bought a small number of shares in another company which it intends to trade.

4 A bank loan has been taken out with a repayment date 5 years hence.

	Current	*Non-current*
A	2 and3	1 and 4
B	3 only	1, 2 and 4
C	1, 2 and 3	4
D	1 and 3	2 and 4

(2 marks)

207 Extracts from the accounting records of Andratx, a company, relating to the year ended 31 December 20X6 are as follows:

Revaluation surplus	$230,000
Ordinary interim dividend paid	$12,000
Profit before tax	$178,000
Estimated tax liability for year	$45,000
8% $1 Preference shares	$100,000
Underprovision for tax in previous year	$5,600
Proceeds of issue of 2,000 $1 ordinary Shares	$5,000
Final ordinary dividend proposed	$30,000

What is the total change reported in the statement of changes in equity for the year?

A $312,400

B $356,000

C $348,000

D $342,400 **(2 marks)**

208 Which of the following statements are true of a preference share?

1 They carry voting rights.

2 Their dividend is paid out in priority to an ordinary dividend.

3 Their dividend is related to profits.

A All 3

B 1 and 2

C 2 and 3

D 2 only **(2 marks)**

209 Bangeroo, a company, issues 100,000 3% $1 redeemable preference shares during the year ended 30 September 20X8 at 98c per share. What is the correct entry to account for this transaction?

		Debit $		*Credit* $
A	Cash	$98,000	Liability	$98,000
B	Cash	$98,000	Share capital	$100,000
	Share premium	$2,000		
C	Cash	$98,000	Share capital	$98,000
D	Cash	$98,000	Share capital	$100,000
	Statement of comprehensive income	$2,000		

(2 marks)

210 The nominal value paid by the shareholder plus further amounts that they have agreed to pay in the future' best describes:

A Paid up share capital

B Called up share capital

C Authorised share capital

D Issued share capital **(2 marks)**

211 Argonaut, a company, issues $400,000 12% loan notes for $380,000 on 1 August 20X6. What accounting entries are required in the year ended 30 September 20X6?

A Dr Cash $400,000
Cr Non-current liabilities $400,000
And
Dr Interest $7,600
Cr Current liabilities $7,600

B Dr Cash $380,000
Cr Non-current liabilities $380,000
And
Dr Interest $8,000
Cr Current liabilities $8,000

C Dr Cash $400,000
Cr Non-current liabilities $400,000
And
Dr Interest $8,000
Cr Current liabilities $8,000

D Dr Cash $380,000
Cr Non-current liabilities $380,000
And
Dr Interest $7,600
Cr Current liabilities $7,600 **(2 marks)**

212 Which of the following are advantages of a bonus issue?

1 It is the cheapest way for a company to raise finance through the issuing of shares.

2 It makes the shares in the company more marketable.

3 The total reserves of the business will increase.

4 Issued share capital is brought more into line with assets employed in the company.

A 2 and 4

B 1 and 2

C 3 and 4

D 1 and 3 **(2 marks)**

213 The share premium and revaluation reserves are revenue reserves, however the accumulated profits and general reserves are capital reserves.

The above statement is:

A True

B False **(1 mark)**

ACCOUNTING STANDARDS

214 Ribblesdale prepares its accounts to a 30 September year end. Its accounts for the year ended 30 September 20X8 are approved on 12 January 20X9 and issued on 20 February 20X9.

Which of the following is an adjusting event after the reporting period?

A A flood destroys inventory which cost $1,700 on 3 December 20X8.

B A credit customer with an outstanding balance at the year end was declared bankrupt on 20 January 20X9.

C Inventory valued at a cost of $800 in the year end accounts was sold for $650 on 11 January 20X9.

D An ordinary dividend of 4c per share was declared on 1 December 20X8. **(2 marks)**

215 Which of the following requires a provision per IAS 37?

1 A retail outlet has a policy of providing refunds over and above the statutory requirement to do so. This policy is well publicised.

2 A customer has made a legal claim against a company, claiming that faulty goods sold to them caused damage to their property. The company's lawyers have advised that the claim will possibly succeed.

A 1 only

B 2 only

C 1 and 2

D Neither **(2 marks)**

216 How should the purchase of a right to manufacture a patented product for the next ten years be accounted for?

A Tangible non-current asset

B Intangible non-current asset

C Current asset **(1 mark)**

217 An intangible asset is:

A an asset with no physical substance

B an asset generated internally by a business

C a purchased asset which has no physical substance

D an asset which can not be used to generate profits in the business **(2 marks)**

218 Which of the following statements about the requirements of IAS 37 *Provisions, Contingent Liabilities and Contingent Assets* are correct?

1 A contingent asset should be disclosed by note if an inflow of economic benefits is probable.

2 No disclosure of a contingent liability is required if the possibility of a transfer of economic benefits arising is remote.

3 Contingent assets must not be recognised in financial statements unless an inflow of economic benefits is virtually certain to arise.

A All three statements are correct

B 1 and 2 only

C 1 and 3 only

D 2 and 3 only **(2 marks)**

219 Which of the following statements are correct according to IAS 10 *Events After the Reporting Period*?

1 Details of all adjusting events must be disclosed by note to the financial statements.

2 A material loss arising from the sale, after the reporting date of inventory valued at cost at the statement of financial position date must be reflected in the financial statements.

3 If the market value of investments falls materially after the reporting date, the details must be disclosed by note.

4 Events after the reporting date are those that occur between the statement of financial position date and the date when the financial statements are approved.

A 1 and 2 only

B 1, 3 and 4

C 2 and 3 only

D 2, 3 and 4 **(2 marks)**

220 The following items have to be considered in finalising the financial statements of Quidditch, a limited liability company:

1 The company gives warranties on its products. The company's statistics show that about 5% of sales give rise to a warranty claim.

2 The company has guaranteed the overdraft of another company. The likelihood of a liability arising under the guarantee is assessed as possible.

What is the correct action to be taken in the financial statements for these items?

	Create a provision	*Disclose by note only*	*No action*
A	1	2	
B		1	2
C	1 and 2		
D		1 and 2	

(2 marks)

221 Geranium is engaged in the following research and development projects:

Project 1 It is applying a new technology to the production of heat resistant fabric. The project is intended to last for a further 18 months after which the fabric will be used in the production of uniforms for the emergency services.

Project 2 It is considering whether a particular substance can be used as an appetite suppressant. If this is the case, it is expected be sold worldwide in chemists and pharmacies.

Project 3 It is developing a material for use in kitchens which is self cleaning and germ resistant. A competitor is currently developing a similar material and for this reason Geranium are unsure whether their project will be completed.

The costs associated with which of these projects can be capitalised?

A Projects 1, 2 and 3

B Projects 1 and 2

C Project 1 only

D Projects 1 and 3 **(2 marks)**

222 Merlot, a limited liability company, is engaged in a number of research and development projects:

Project A A project to investigate the properties of a chemical compound

Project B A project to develop a new process which will save time in the production of widgets. This project was started on 1 January 20X5 and met the capitalisation criteria on 31 August 20X5.

Project C A development project which was completed on 30 June 20X5. Related costs in the statement of financial position at the start of the year were $290,000. Production and sales of the new product commenced on 1 September and are expected to last 36 months.

Costs for the year ended 31 December 20X5 are as follows:

	$
Project A	34,000
Project B costs to 31 August	78,870
Project B costs from 31 August	27,800
Project C costs to 30 June	19,800

What amount is expensed to the statement of comprehensive income in respect of these projects in the year ended 31 December 20X5?

A $147,292

B $68,422

C $66,222

D $145,092 **(2 marks)**

223 Romulus, a company, makes two changes to accounting practice at the end of 20X7:

1 It changes the way in which it depreciates motor vehicles from 20% straight line to 25% reducing balance.

2 It starts to capitalise interest costs where allowed in accordance with the relevant standard. Previously it had adopted a policy of writing off all interest costs to the statement of comprehensive income.

What is the correct way to account for these two changes?

	1	*2*	
A	Do not adjust opening reserves	Do not adjust opening reserves	
B	Do not adjust opening reserves	Adjust opening reserves	
C	Adjust opening reserves	Adjust opening reserves	
D	Adjust opening reserves	Do not adjust opening reserves	**(2 marks)**

224 Details of two of Clooney's transactions in the year ended 31 August 20X7 are as follows:

1 It has sold a food processing machine to a customer, Pitt. The machine has been delivered and Clooney will undertake specialist installation within the next month.

2 It has sold a number of food mixers to another customer, Damon, on credit. These have been delivered but Damon has not yet paid

For which of the transactions should revenue be recognised?

A 1 only

B 2 only

C Both 1 and 2

D Neither 1 nor 2 **(2 marks)**

225 Which of the following is not a condition that must be met in order to record revenue from the rendering of services?

A The amount can be measured reliably

B Stage of completion of the work can be measured reliably

C Costs incurred for the transaction can be measured reliably

D The seller has passed on effective control of the service being performed **(2 marks)**

STATEMENT OF CASH FLOWS

226 Extracts from the accounts of Deuce showed balances as follows:

	20X9	*20X8*
$1 Share capital	300,000	120,000
Share premium	260,000	100,000

A bonus issue of 1 share for every 12 held at the 20X8 year end occurred during the year and loan notes of $300,000 were issued at par. Interest of $12,000 was paid during the year.

What is the net cash inflow from financing activities?

A $480,000

B $605,000

C $617,000

D $640,000 **(2 marks)**

227 Nobus is producing its statement of cash flows for the year ended 31 December 20X5. The accountant has identified the following balances in the financial statements:

	$
Interest accrual b/f	4,900
Interest accrual c/f	1,200
Interest payable	20,000
Interest receivable	13,000
Preference dividend payable b/f	120,000
Preference dividends payable c/f	140,000
Dividends (statement of changes in equity)	600,000

What is the net cash flow from investing activities?

A ($10,700)

B $13,000

C ($603,700)

D ($590,700) **(2 marks)**

228 Which of the following items could appear as items in a company's statement of cash flows?

1 A bonus issue of shares.

2 A rights issue of shares.

3 The revaluation of non-current assets.

4 Dividends paid.

A All four items

B 1, 3 and 4 only

C 2 and 4 only **(1 mark)**

229 A draft statement of cash flows contains the following:

	$m
Profit before tax	22
Depreciation	8
Increase in inventories	(4)
Decrease in receivables	(3)
Increase in payables	(2)
Net cash inflow from operating activities	21

Which of the following corrections needs to be made to the calculations?

1 Depreciation should be deducted, not added.

2 Increase in inventories should be added, not deducted.

3 Decrease in receivables should be added, not deducted.

4 Increase in payables should be added, not deducted.

A 1 and 2

B 1 and 3

C 2 and 4

D 3 and 4 **(2 marks)**

230 Where, in a company's financial statements complying with International accounting standards, should you find the proceeds of non-current assets sold during the period?

A Statement of cash flows and statement of financial position

B Statement of changes in equity and statement of financial position

C Statement of comprehensive income and cash flow statement

D Statement of cash flows only **(2 marks)**

231 The figures below have been prepared for inclusion in the statement of cash flows of Bamboo.

	$
Tax and dividends paid	87,566
Increase in payables	13,899
Decrease in inventory	8,900
Redemption of loans	300,000
Increase in receivables	6,555
Reduction in cash and cash equivalents	3,211
Depreciation charge	10,600
Payments to acquire non-current assets	47,999
Proceeds from sale of non-current assets	13,100

What is the cash generated from operations?

A $331,688

B $338,110

C $425,676

D $419,254 **(2 marks)**

232 A business's bank balance increased by $750,000 during its last financial year. During the same period it issued shares, raising $1 million and repaid a loan of $750,000. It purchased non-current assets for $200,000 and charged depreciation of $100,000. Receivables and inventory increased by $575,000.

Its profit for the year was:

A $1,175,000

B $1,275,000

C $1,325,000

D $1,375,000 **(2 marks)**

233 A business had non-current assets with a book value of $50,000 at the start of the financial year. During the year the business sold assets that had cost $4,000 and had been depreciated by $1,500. Depreciation for the year was $9,000. The book value of assets at the end of the financial year was $46,000. How much cash has been invested in non-current assets during the year?

A $4,000

B $7,500

C $9,000

D $10,000 **(2 marks)**

234 A business has made a profit of $8,000 but its bank balance has fallen by $5,000. This could be due to:

A depreciation of $3,000 and an increase in inventories of $10,000

B depreciation of $6,000 and the repayment of a loan of $7,000

C depreciation of $12,000 and the purchase of new non-current assets for $25,000

D the disposal of a non-current asset for $13,000 less than its book value **(2 marks)**

235 A company made a profit for the year of $18,750, after accounting for depreciation of $1,250.

During the year, non-current assets were purchased for $8,000, receivables increased by $1,000, inventories decreased by $1,800 and payables increased by $350.

The increase in cash and bank balances during the year was:

A $10,650

B $10,850

C $12,450

D $13,150 **(2 marks)**

236 A statement of cash flows prepared in accordance with the indirect method reconciles profit before tax to cash generated from operations.

Which of the following lists of items consists only of items that would be ADDED to profit before tax?

A Decrease in inventory, depreciation, profit on sale of non-current assets

B Increase in payables, decrease in receivables, profit on sale of non-current assets

C Loss on sale of non-current assets, depreciation, increase in receivables

D Decrease in receivables, increase in payables, loss on sale of non-current assets

(2 marks)

237 In relation to statements of cash flows, which, if any, of the following are correct?

Statement

1 The direct method of calculating net cash from operating activities leads to a different figure from that produced by the indirect method, but this is balanced elsewhere in the statement of cash flows.

2 A company making high profits must necessarily have a net cash inflow from operating activities.

3 Profits and losses on disposals of non-current assets appear as items under investing activities in the statement of cash flows.

A Statement 1 only

B Statement 2 only

C Statement 3 only

D None of the statements

(2 marks)

238 The movement on the plant and machinery account for X is shown below:

	$
Cost b/f	10,000
Additions	2,000
Disposals	(3,000)
Cost c/f	9,000
Depreciation b/f	2,000
Charge for the year	1,000
Disposals	(1,500)
Depreciation c/f	1,500
Carrying value b/f	8,000
Carrying value c/f	7,500

The profit on the sale of the machine was $500. What figures would appear in the statement of cash flows of X under the heading of 'Investing activities'?

A Movement on plant account $500 and profit on disposal of $500

B Movement on plant account $500 and proceeds on sale of plant $2,000

C Purchase of plant $2,000 and profit on disposal of $500

D Purchase of plant $2,000 and proceeds on sale of plant $2,000

(2 marks)

239 Which of the following is not an advantage of the statement of cash flows?

A It highlights the effect of non-cash transactions

B It helps an assessment of the liquidity off a business

C The numbers within it cannot be manipulated through the adoption of beneficial accounting policies

D It helps users to estimate future cash flows **(2 marks)**

240 Grainger is calculating its cash flow using the direct method, and has found the following information:

Cash sales	$212,500
Cash purchases	$4,600
Cash expenses	$11,200
Payables at start of year	$12,300
Payables at end of year	$14,300
Credit purchases	$123,780
Wages and salaries due at start of year	$1,500
Wages and salaries due at end of year	$2,300
Wages and salaries expense	$34,600
Inventory at start of year	$23,000
Inventory at end of year	$17,800

All sales are made for cash. What is the cash generated from operations by Grainger?

A $35,520

B $46,320

C $74,920

D $41,120 **(2 marks)**

241 Howard, a limited liability company, provides the following extracts from the statement of financial position for the years ended 31December:

	20X6	*20X7*
	$000	$000
Accumulated profits	72,000	82,000
10% Loan notes	30,000	40,000
Tax payable	12,000	15,000
Dividends payable	1,200	1,600

(All declared and proposed **before** the year end.)

There was no adjustment for under/over provision for tax in the year ended 31 December 20X7. No interim dividends were paid during the year. The additional 10% loan notes were issued on 1 January 20X7.

What is the operating profit (profit before interest and tax) for the year ended 31 December 20X7?

A $29,600

B $27,200

C $30,600

D $102,600 **(2 marks)**

REGULATORY FRAMEWORK

242 The Standards Advisory Council are responsible for:

(1) issuing guidance in relation to emerging issues.

(2) advising the IASB on major standard-setting projects.

A 1 and 2

B 1 only

C 2 only

D Neither 1 nor two **(2 marks)**

243 Which of the following assumptions underlie the Framework for the presentation and preparation of financial statements?

A Accruals and consistency

B Prudence and going concern

C Accruals and going concern

D Consistency and prudence **(2 marks)**

244 Which of the following are true?

1 International accounting standards are effective only if adopted by national regulatory bodies.

2 Accounting standards provide guidance on accounting for all types of transaction.

A 1 only

B 2 only

C 1 and 2

D Neither **(2 marks)**

245 Which one of the following statements is correct?

A The prudence concept requires assets to be understated and liabilities to be overstated

B To comply with the law, the legal form of a transaction must always be reflected in financial statements

C If a non-current asset initially recognised at cost is revalued, the surplus must be credited in the statement of cash flows

D In times of rising prices, the use of historical cost accounting tends to understate assets and overstate profits **(2 marks)**

246 Which of the following characteristics of financial information contribute to reliability according to the IASB's Framework for the Preparation and Presentation of Financial Statements?

1 Completeness.

2 Prudence.

3 Neutrality.

4 Faithful representation.

A All four items

B 1, 2 and 3 only

C 1, 2 and 4 only

D 2, 3 and 4 only **(2 marks)**

247 An item of inventory which had cost $5 was sold for $7. It cost the company $6 to replace the item. At the time of the sale the $6 was the item's:

A historical cost

B net realisable value

C economic value

D current cost **(2 marks)**

248 The accounting concept which dictates that non-current assets should be valued at cost less accumulated depreciation, rather than at their enforced saleable value, is:

A Understandability

B Relevance

C Comparability

D Going concern **(2 marks)**

249 Inventories should be valued at the lower of cost and net realisable value. Which ONE of the following accounting concepts governs this?

A Comparability

B Prudence

C Going concern **(1 mark)**

250 Which of the following pairs of accounting concepts are most likely to be in conflict with one another?

A Comparability and understandability

B Accruals basis and going concern

C Comparability and reliability

D Relevance and reliability **(2 marks)**

251 Why should financial statements be prepared on a consistent basis?

A To make it easier to compare results from one year to the next

B To make the financial statements easier to understand **(1 mark)**

252 Which of the following statements is most accurate about the historical cost concept?

A Records transactions from past years

B Fails to take account of changing price levels over time

C Values assets at their cost to the business, irrespective of any depreciation or other loss in value

D Is no longer used in modern accounting systems **(1 mark)**

253 In times of falling prices, the historical cost convention:

A understates asset values and profits

B understates asset values and overstates profits

C overstates asset values and profits

D overstates asset values and understates profits **(1 mark)**

254 Who issues International Financial Reporting Standards?

A The IASC Foundation

B The International Financial Reporting Interpretations Committee

C The International Accounting Standards Board **(1 mark)**

255 Which of the following statements about the Framework are true?

1 The Framework is an accounting standard.

2 It assists in harmonising accounting practice.

3 It assists national standard setters in developing national standards.

4 It assists users of the accounts to interpret financial statements.

A 1 and 2

B 2, 3 and 4

C All 4

D 1 and 3 **(2 marks)**

256 Which of the following are advantages of historical cost accounting?

1 It maintains financial and physical capital.

2 The statement of financial position shows the value of the business.

3 Reported amounts are objectively verifiable.

4 The profit concept is well understood.

A 3 and 4

B 1 and 2

C 1 and 3

D 2 and 4 **(2 marks)**

Section 2

ANSWERS TO PRACTICE QUESTIONS

INTRODUCTION TO ACCOUNTING

1 D

- The directors of a company run the company, however are not liable for its losses.
- A sole trader business is owned and operated by the proprietor (sole trader)
- Partners are jointly and severally liable for any losses of the business.
- A company is owned by the shareholders (members) and run by the directors/ management team.

2 B

Management accounts are:

- Sufficiently detailed for management to control the business and plan for the future.
- Normally prepared monthly (on a rolling basis).
- Not mandatory.
- Based on past performance as well as budgets and forecasts.
- Relevant to managers.

3 C

- An employee is interested in whether a business will continue into the future in order to assess their job security. This is a prime concern of an employee.
- Employees may be able to invest in shares in the company they work for, in which case profitability will be of interest to them. This is, however, not always the case.
- Employees may also be interested in the effect of the business on the local environment and community, and the performance of competitors however these are generally secondary concerns.

4 A

Management require very detailed information in order to make informed decisions with regard to operations (e.g. whether to shut down a particular product line or source new suppliers).

Other parties need far less detail:

- Investors are interested in profitability and the security of their investment.
- The government is interested in profits (for tax purposes) and sales performance (in order to assess how the economy is performing).
- Lenders are interested in whether a business is solvent and able to repay their debt.

5 A

- Accounting involves recording transactions as they occur and then summarising them in the form of the financial statements.
- Financial accounting describes the production of accounts for external use.

6 C

7 C

Both financial and management accounts are equally accurate.

STATEMENT OF FINANCIAL POSITION AND INCOME STATEMENT

8 B

	$	$
Sales (β)		25,600
Cost of sales		
Opening inventory	1,500	
Purchases	12,950	
Inventory drawings	(75)	
Closing inventory	(900)	
		(13,475)
Gross profit		12,125

9 B

- The definition of an asset requires that it is controlled by an entity. Whether the item is owned outright or paid for are irrelevant as long as control is achieved.
- An item owed by an entity is a liability.

10 A

Opening net assets + capital injections + profit – drawings = closing net assets

Opening net assets + $9,800 + $8,000 – $4,200 = $19,000

Opening net assets = Opening capital = $5,400

11 D

Capital = net assets

- If a supplier is paid by cheque, assets reduce as do liabilities, therefore there is no change to net assets.
- If raw materials or non-current assets are purchased on credit, assets increase as do liabilities; again there is no change to net assets.
- If wages are paid in cash, assets decrease (the other effect is to reduce profits which in turn reduces capital).

12 B

The loan was included as a current liability, but should be treated as a non-current liability. Correcting the error will reduce total current liabilities, and this will increase net current assets (= current assets minus current liabilities).

13 B

Profit is the increase in net assets between the beginning and end of the period, plus drawings taken out of the business, minus new equity introduced in the period (which is not profit).

14 C

The separate business entity concept means that accounting information should only relate to the business, not the owner of the business. Therefore goods taken by the owner must be treated as drawings and removed from the inventory of the business.

15 D

Current assets	$	*Current liabilities*	$
Receivables	23,800	Overdraft	3250
Allowances for receivables	(1,500)	Payables	31,050
Inventory	12,560	Rent accrual	1,200
Petty cash	150	Loan	25,000
	35,010		60,500

- The bank statement shows a debit balance, indicating an overdraft (from the bank's perspective, they are owed money by Andrew).
- The first instalment of the loan (25%) is due within 12 months and so shown as a current liability.

16 A

Assets	=	Liabilities	+	Capital
At start of week:				
15,700	=	11,200	+	4,500(β)
1 May				
+300		+ 300		+ 1,400
+1,400				
3 May				
–750				– 750
4 May				
–400				– 400
7 May				
+1,200				+ 1,200
–600				– 600
At end of week:				
16,850	=	11,500	+	5,350

DOUBLE ENTRY BOOKKEEPING

17 B

- The computer does not qualify as inventory drawings as it is for the use of Oscar's daughter in her role as administrator to the business.
- The computer is being transferred from inventory to non-current assets by debiting the non-current assets account. It is no longer part of cost of sales and is removed from cost of sales by a credit.

18 B

- Drawings, carriage outwards (an expense), prepayments, Carriage inwards (expense) and opening inventory are all debit balances.
- Accruals, rental income and purchase returns are all credit balances.

19 C

20 C

21 D

	$	$
Sales		256,800
Cost of sales		
Opening inventory	13,400	
Purchases	145,000	
Carriage in	2,300	
Closing inventory	(14,200)	
		(146,500)
Gross profit		110,300
Expenses		(76,000)
Discount allowed		(1,950)
Discount received		3,900
Net profit		36,250

22 B

Bank

	$		$
Balance b/f	1,780	Drawings (4 × $200)	800
Receipt after discount	570		
Receipt from customer	400		
Bankings	1,200	Balance c/f	3,150
	3,950		3,950

Settlement discounts are given if a credit customer pays within a certain time. If a $30 settlement discount is taken, then the net amount of $570 must have been received during the month.

23 D

Bank

	$		$
Returns of goods purchased for cash	50	Overdraft at start of month	1,340
Rental income	1,300	Payments to credit suppliers	990
Receipts from customers	4,400	Reimbursement of petty cash float	45
		Payment of electricity bill	700
		Balance c/f	2,675
	5,750		5,750

24 C

INVENTORY

25 A

- The inventory should be valued at the lower of cost and NRV.
- Cost is $500.
- NRV is $1,200 – $250 = $950.
- The correct valuation is therefore $500.

26 A

Opening inventory + units purchased		440
Units sold		(290)
Closing inventory (units)		150
FIFO Closing inventory: 150 units @ $2.78		$417
AVCO	Weighted average cost	$
	100 units @ $2.52	252
	140 units @ $2.56	358
	200 units @ $2.78	556
	440	1,166
Average cost per unit		1,166 / 440 = $2.65
Closing inventory: 150 units @ $2.65		$397.50
FIFO higher by (417 – 397.50)		$19.50

The periodic weighted requires the total cost of the inventory to be divided by the total units in the period to determine the weighted average cost for the period. This weighted average figure will then be used to value the inventory.

The continuous weighted method requires the weighted average to be calculated every time there is a purchase.

27 B

- If prices have fallen during the year, AVCO will give a higher value of closing inventory than FIFO, which values goods for resale at the latest prices.
- Where the value of closing inventory is higher, profits are higher.

28 D

- The number of units held at the year end is 1,180 (1,200 – 20)

The sale on 31 December provides evidence of a net realisable value $2 below cost. Therefore each unit should be valued at its net realisable value:

1,180 units × $48 = $56,640

29 C

- Inventory should be valued at the lower of cost and net realisable value. Replacement cost is irrelevant.

30 C

- Where inventory is included in purchases at cost and closing inventory at cost, the effect on profit is nil (the same amount is both a debit and a credit in the income statement).
- In this case, only the credit is recorded (closing inventory). Therefore profit is overstated by the cost of the fabric.
- Inventory is neither under nor overstated, since the inclusion of the fabric is correct.

31 A

- Inventory drawings are credited to purchases in order to remove them from cost of sales, as these goods have not been sold.

32 B

At the year end:

1. Opening inventory must be removed from the statement of financial position inventory account (a credit) and expensed to the income statement as part of cost of sales (a debit).
2. Closing inventory must be debited on to the statement of financial position as an asset and removed from the cost of sales (a credit).

33 B

	$
Value at 7 July 20X6	38,950
Sales since year end (100/125 × $6,500)	5,200
Purchase since year end	(4,250)
Value at 30 June 20X6	39,900

34 B

	Items	Unit value	
		$	$
Opening inventory	6	15	90
January: purchases	10	19.80	198
	16	18	288
February: sales	(10)	18	(180)
	6	18	108
March: purchases	20	24.50	490
	26	23	598
March: sales	(5)	23	(115)
	21	23	483

	$
Sales (15 × $30)	450
Cost of sales ($180 + $115)	(295)
Gross profit	155

35 C

Date		*Units*	*Unit value*	*Inventory value*
			$	$
1 October	Opening inventory	60		720
8 October	Purchase 40 units at $15	40		600
14 October	Purchase 50 units at $18	50		900
		150	14.80	2,220
21 October	Sold 75 units: cost	(75)	14.80	(1,110)
31 October	Closing inventory	75	14.80	1,110

36 A

The net realisable value of inventory items is the selling price less the 4% commission payable.

	NRV	*Lower of cost or NRV*
	$	$
Henry VII	2,784	2,280
Dissuasion	3,840	3,840
John Bunion	1,248	1,248
		7,368

37 D

The closing inventory of 12 items (15 – 5 + 10 – 8) comprise

	$
10 items at $3.50 each	35.00
2 items at $3 each	6.00
Cost on a FIFO basis is	41.00

38 B

If the inventory was not included in the original count of closing inventory, closing inventory will be increased by $1,000 (the lower of cost and net realisable value). Since closing inventory is $1,000 higher, the cost of sales is $1,000 lower and profit $1,000 higher.

39 B

	Net realisable value	*Lower of cost or NRV*	*Units*	*Value*
	$	$		$
Basic	8	6	200	1,200
Super	8	8	250	2,000
Luxury	10	10	150	1,500
Total value				4,700

40 A

When prices are rising, FIFO will give a higher valuation for closing inventory, because the closing inventory will consist of the most recently-purchased items. Higher closing inventory means lower cost of sales and higher profit.

SALES TAX

41 A

		$
Price	600	
Less: trade discount (5% × £600)	(30)	
	570	
Less: Cash/settlement discount (3% × $570)	(17.10)	
	552.90	
Sales tax at 17.5 × $552.90	=	$96.76

Sales tax is always charged on the selling price net of:

- actual trade (bulk buy) discounts given
- settlement (prompt payment) discounts, regardless of whether they are taken.

42 C

Sales tax

	$		$
		Balance b/f	23,778
Tax on purchases		Tax on sales	
$\frac{17.5\%}{117.5\%}$ × $590,790	87,990	17.5% × $800,000	140,000
Balance c/f	75,788		
	163,778		163,778
		Balance b/f	75,788

43 B

Sales tax

	$		$
Tax on purchases (input tax) ($18,000 × 17.5%)	3,150.0	Tax on sales (output tax) ($27,612.5 × 17.5/117.5)	4,112.5
Balance c/f	962.5		
	4,112.5		4,112.5
		Balance b/f	962.5

44 C

	$
Sales net of sales tax	90,000
Purchases net of sales tax	(72,000)
	18,000
Tax payable @ 10%	$1,800

As sales exceed purchases, the excess sales tax is payable to the tax authorities.

45 D

Sales tax

	$		$
Tax on purchases	6,000	Balance b/f	3,400
Bank	2,600	Tax on sales	10,500
Balance c/f	5,300		
	13,900		13,900
		Balance b/f	5,300

Tax on sales (outputs) = 17.5% × $60,000 = $10,500

Tax on purchases (inputs) = (17.5/117.5) × $40,286 = $6,000

46 B

Sales are recorded exclusive of sales tax in the income statement.

47 B

The receivables account should be debited with the full amount payable, including the tax. The entry in the sales account should be for the sales value excluding sales tax. Sales tax payable to the tax authorities should be credited to the sales tax account (liability = credit balance).

48 A

The receivables account should be credited with the full amount of the sales return, including the tax. The Sales returns account should be debited with the value of the returns excluding the sales tax. The sales tax account should be debited with the amount of tax on the returns (since the tax is no longer payable).

49 C

The supplier is owed the full amount of the invoice, including the sales tax, so the credit entry in the supplier account must be $9,200. The non-current asset account is recorded at cost excluding the sales tax. The input tax is recoverable, so debit the sales tax account with $1,200.

50 A

- If input tax (tax on purchases) exceeds output tax (tax on sales), the difference is recoverable from the tax authorities.
- Sales and purchases are reported net of sales tax.
- Sales tax cannot be recovered on certain expenses (such as client entertaining) and purchases (such as cars).

ACCRUALS AND PREPAYMENTS

51 A

Rental income (property 1 and 2)

	$		$
Balance b/f	5,400	Balance b/f	12,300
Income statement rental income (β)	453,600	Cash received (280,000 +160,000)	440,000
Balance c/f	6,700	Balance c/f	13,400
	465,700		465,700
Balance b/f	13,400	Balance b/f	6,700

52 D

Rental income

	$		$
Balance b/f	42,300	Balance b/f	102,600
Income statement (β)	858,600	Cash received	838,600
Balance c/f	88,700	Balance c/f	48,400
	989,600		989,600

53 A

		$
Income statement	9/12 × $10,800	8,100
	3/12 × $12,000	3,000
		11,100
Statement of financial position prepayment	9/12 × $12,000	9,000

54 D

Income statement (5/12 × $24,000) + (7/12 × $30,000) =$27,500

Statement of financial position $7,500 paid on 1 January therefore amount prepaid by tenant is:

2/3 × $7,500 = $5,000. For Vine this is prepaid/deferred income, i.e. income received in advance – a liability.

55 A

Motor expenses

		$		$
Balance b/f (insurance)		80	Balance b/f (petrol)	95
Cash paid	– petrol	95		
	– other bills	245	Income statement (β)	385
Balance c/f (petrol)		120	Balance c/f (insurance)	60
		540		540

The insurance prepayment covers 4 months as at the start of September. Therefore there must be a prepayment of 3 months at the end of September.

56 A

Charge to income statement $1,800 × 7/12 = $1,050

Prepayment $1,800 × 5/12 = $750

57 C

The accrual for May and June 20X3 is assumed to be 2/3 × $840 = $560.

Electricity expenses

	$		$
Bank	600	Opening balance b/f	300
Bank	720		
Bank	900		
Bank	840		
Closing balance c/f	560	Income statement	3,320
	3,620		3,620

58 C

The premium for the year 1 July 20X2 to 30 June 20X3 was $13,200 × 1/1.1 = $12,000

Income statement charge:

6 months at $12,000 plus 6 months at $13,200 = $6,000 + $6,600 = $12,600

59 B

The charge in the income statement will be the amount of interest incurred from 1 January (when the loan was taken out) to 30 September (the year end) i.e. 9/12 × 12% × $100,000 = $9,000. This represents three interest payments.

However, as only two interest payments were made (1 April and 1 July) the third payment due to be made on 1 October, which relates to the three months to 30 September, will be accrued: 3/12 × 12% × $100,000 = $3,000.

60 C

	$
Prepayment brought forward at the start of the year	10,000
Payment during the year	36,000
	46,000
Less: Prepayment carried forward at the year end (7 months, therefore $36,000 × 7/12)	(21,000)
Charge for insurance in the income statement	25,000

61 B

- Accrued income is income not yet received for a service already provided (income received in arrears). The correct double entry to record accrued income is:

Dr Accrued income (statement of financial position)

Cr Income (income statement)

It therefore increases rather than decreases profit.

IRRECOVERABLE DEBTS AND ALLOWANCES FOR RECEIVABLES

62 D

Receivables ledger control account

	$		$
Balance b/f	34,500	Cash received	229,900
Credit sales (β)	278,090	Contra	1,200
		Discounts allowed	17,890
		Irrecoverable debts	18,600
		Balance c/f	45,000
	312,590		312,590
Balance b/f	45,000		

Total sale = Credit sales + Cash sales

= $278,090 + $24,000

= $302,090

Note:

- Discounts received are relevant to the payables ledger control account.
- The double entry for the increase in allowance for receivables is:

Dr Irrecoverable debts expense	12,500
Cr Allowance for receivables	12,500

63 B

Receivables ledger control account

	$		$
Balance b/f	84,700	Contra with payables ledger control account	5,000
Credit sales	644,000	Irrecoverable debts	4,300
		Discounts allowed	30,780
		Cash received from credit customers	595,000
		Balance c/f	93,620
	728,700		728,700

- The double entry for a contra is Dr payables ledger control account (payables) and Cr receivables ledger control account (receivables).
- Discounts received are relevant to payables not receivables.
- Cash sales should not feature in the receivables ledger control account.
- The correct double entry for the increase in the allowance for receivables is Dr irrecoverable debts expense and Cr allowance for receivables.

64 A

		Allowance	*Expense*
	$	$	$
Receivables balance (draft)	58,200		
Irrecoverable debts	(8,900)		8,900
	49,300		
Specific allowance: Carroll	(1,350)	1,350	
Juffs	(750)	750	
	47,200		
General allowance at 3% × $47,200		1,416	
Allowance c/f		3,516	
Allowance b/f		5,650	
Decrease in allowance		2,134	(2,134)
Total expense			6,766

65 B

Receivables ledger control account

	$		$
Balance b/f (W)	13,150		
Sales	125,000	Cash	115,500
		Irrecoverable debts	7,100
		Balance c/f	15,550
	138,150		138,150

	b/f	*c/f*
	$	$
Gross receivables	13,150	15,550
Allowance	(1,150)	(2,100)
Net receivables	12,000	13,450

66 B

- The write off of debts will reduce the gross receivables balance by $72,000 to $766,000.
- The allowance is to be adjusted to $60,000 (hence an adjustment of $12,000).
- The net balance is therefore $766,000 less $60,000, i.e. $706,000.

67 A

Year end receivables	5% × $7,000,000	=	$350,000
Year end allowance for receivables	4% × $350,000	=	$14,000
Allowance at start of year	100/120 × $14,000	=	$11,667
Increase in allowance		=	**$2,333**

Irrecoverable debts expense

	$		$
Write off of irrecoverable debts	3,200	Recovery of irrecoverable debts	450
Increase in allowance	2,333	Income statement (β)	5,083
	5,533		5,533

68 A

Trade receivables

	$		$
Balance b/f	10,000	Receipts	90,000
Sales	100,000	Discounts allowed	800
Bad debts recovered	1,000	Balance c/f	20,200
	111,000		111,000

69 A

When a debt is written off as bad, the transaction is recorded as:

Dr Irrecoverable debts account (expense)

Cr Receivable account.

Any subsequent change to the allowance for receivables should be dealt with as a separate matter.

70 A

- Cash sales do not affect receivables.
- Discounts received affect payables, not receivables.
- The allowance for receivables does not affect the amount of receivables, but specific bad debts written off do affect receivables.

Receivables

	$		$
Balance b/f	37,500	Discounts allowed	15,750
Sales (credit)	357,500	Irrecoverable debts written off	10,500
		Bank (β)	329,750
		Balance c/f	39,000
	395,000		395,000

71 A

- Receivables (5% of $2 million) = $100,000.
- Required allowance for receivables (4% of $100,000) = $4,000.
- Current allowance for receivables = $4,000 × ¾ = $3,000.
- Increase in allowance = $1,000.
- An increase in the allowance for receivables reduces profits.

72 A

	$
Irrecoverable debts written off (800 + 550)	1,350
Irrecoverable debt recovered	(350)
Reduction in allowance for receivables	(200)
Charge to income statement	800

73 B

The allowance for receivables will reduce the book value of receivables. An increase in an allowance for receivables will therefore reduce net current assets.

74 A

	$	$	$
Receivables balance		230,000	
Specific allowance – Emily		(450)	450
– Lulu		(980)	980
		228,570	
General allowance @ 5% of $228,570			11,429
Total allowance at end of year			12,859
Allowance b/f			(11,700)
Increase in allowance = Dr to income statement			1,159

75 D

The provision of credit will not improve the cash flow position of the business, rather it may result in a deterioration of cash flow. This is particularly true as some customers will be late in paying and others will not pay at all.

76 C

An aged receivables analysis is a list of how much each credit customer owes and how old their debt is. It enables the credit control function to identify which customers to chase, and also helps in the calculation of the allowance for receivables at the year end.

NON-CURRENT ASSETS

77 C

Asset register	$	*Ledger accounts*	$
Carrying value per question	85,600	Carrying value per question	130,000
Addition of land	30,000	Disposal at carrying value	(14,400)
	115,600		115,600

78 A

		$
1.1.X4	Cost	235,000
	Depreciation at 30%	(70,500)
y/e 31.12.X4	Carrying value	164,500
	Depreciation at 30%	(49,350)
y/e 31.12.X5	Carrying value	115,150
	Depreciation at 20%	(34,545)
y/e 31.12.X6	Carrying value	80,605
	Accumulated depreciation (70,500 + 49,350 + 34,545)	154,395

Therefore

(1) Uplift cost account to valuation

Dr Cost $65,000

(2) Remove depreciation to date

Dr Accumulated depreciation $154,395

(3) Send the balance to the revaluation reserve

Cr Revaluation reserve $219,395

79 D

A non-current asset register is a detailed schedule of non-current assets, and is not another name for non-current asset ledger accounts in the general ledger.

80 A

81 B

			$
Depreciation on additions:	20% × $48,000 × 6/12	=	4,800
Depreciation on disposals:	20% × $84,000 × 9/12	=	12,600
Depreciation on other assets:	20% × (960,000 – 84,000)	=	175,200
			192,600

82 C

	$
Cost of plant	48,000
Delivery	400
Modifications	2,200
	50,600

The warranty cost cannot be capitalised. This is a revenue expense which must be debited to the income statement.

83 B

		$
Year 1	Cost	2,400.0
	Depreciation at 20%	(480.0)
Year 2	Carrying value	1,920.0
	Depreciation at 20%	(384.0)
Year 3	Carrying value	1,536.0
	Depreciation at 20%	(307.2)
Year 4	Carrying value	1,228.8
	Sale proceeds	1,200.0
	Loss on disposal	(28.8)

84 B

	$	$
Original balance		125,000
Net book value of assets sold:		
Proceeds	9,000	
Less: Profit	(2,000)	
		(7,000)
Adjusted balance		118,000

85 C

A non-current asset should be measured initially at its cost. 'Cost' means the amounts incurred to acquire the asset and bring it into working condition for its intended use. These include the purchase cost, initial delivery and handling costs, installation costs and professional fees. Costs of testing whether the asset is working properly may be included, but costs of staff training are not.

	$
Purchase cost of machine	80,000
Installation	5,000
Testing	1,000
	86,000

86 A

	$
Cost	5,000
Year 1 (20% × 5,000)	(1,000)
Year 2 (20% × 4,000)	(800)
Year 3 (20% × 3,200)	(640)
Carrying value at time of disposal	2,560
Sale proceeds	2,200
Loss on disposal	360

Note: The residual value does not impact reducing balance calculations of depreciation.

87 C

	$m
Non-current assets at cost	10.40
Accumulated depreciation	(0.12)
Carrying value	10.28
Revaluation amount	15.00
Transfer to revaluation reserve	4.72

88 D

Painting and replacing windows are maintenance and repairs, and so are classified as 'revenue expenditure' and must be expensed through the income statement. The purchase of a car for resale means that the car is an item of inventory for the business, not a non-current asset. Legal fees incurred in purchasing a building are included in the cost of the building, and so are part of the non-current asset cost, i.e. capital expenditure.

89 D

Disposals account

	$		$
Cost	12,000	Accumulated depreciation (3yrs × 20% × $12,000)	7,200
Profit (β)	200	Proceeds (part exchange allowance)	5,000
	12,200		12,200

90 C

	Cost	*Accum dep'n*	*Carrying value*
	$000	$000	$000
Opening balance	860	397	
Disposal	(80)	(43)	
	780	354	
Purchase	180		
	960		
Depreciation (10%)		96	
		450	
CV = 960 – 450			510

91 C

92 C

1 Jan – 30 June: 3% of $380,000 × 6/12 = $5,700

1 July – 31 December: 3% of $450,000 × 6/12 = $6,750

Charge for the year: $5,700 + $6,750 = $12,450

93 D

Do not include the road tax in the cost of the car. Road tax is a revenue expense item.

	$
Cost of asset	10,000
Depreciation 20X1 (25%)	(2,500)
	7,500
Depreciation 20X2 (25%)	(1,875)
	5,625
Depreciation 20X3 (25%)	(1,406)
	4,219
Depreciation 20X4 (25%)	(1,055)
Net book value at time of disposal	3,164
Disposal value	5,000
Profit on disposal	1,836

94 D

The reducing balance method charges more depreciation in earlier years than in later years. It is therefore appropriate to use for assets such as motor vehicles that lose a large part of their value in the earlier years of their life.

95 C

Annual depreciation = $(40,000 – 10,000)/6 years = $5,000.

The machine was held for four years before disposal, giving accumulated depreciation of 4 × $5,000 = $20,000.

When the machine was sold, its carrying value was $40,000 – $20,000 = $20,000. It was sold for $15,000, giving a loss on disposal of $5,000.

	$
Accumulated depreciation	20,000
Loss on disposal	5,000
Total charged over the life of the machine	25,000

96 B

Initial depreciation charge p.a. $\frac{\$20,000 - \$500}{10 \text{ years}}$ = $1,950

Carrying value at date of change $20,000 – $1,950 = $18,050

New depreciation charge (for y/e 30 June X9 onwards) $\frac{\$18,050}{5 \text{ yrs}}$ = $3,610

Note that the revision of estimations takes place in the year ended 30 June 20X9 before the depreciation for that year is charged.

FROM TRIAL BALANCE TO FINANCIAL STATEMENTS

97 C

	$	$
Plant and machinery	89,000	
Property	120,000	
Inventory	4,600	
Payables		6,300
Receivables	5,900	
Bank overdraft		790
Loan		50,000
Capital		100,000
Drawings	23,000	
Sales		330,000
Purchases	165,000	
Sales returns	7,000	
Discounts allowed	3,200	
Sundry expenses	73,890	
Discounts received (β)		4,500
	491,590	491,590

98 B

Where a trial balance agrees, this does not confirm that no errors have been made in the accounting records. Only those errors resulting from a journal entry without an equal debit and credit will be highlighted by the trial balance.

99 C

All three are limitations of a trial balance:

- Figures in the trial balance are not necessarily the final figures to be reported in the financial statements; they are subject to year end adjustments.
- Errors of commission (where an entry has been posted to the wrong account) are not identified by the trial balance since an equal debit and credit entry are still posted.
- Although a trial balance can identify if double entry has broken down, it does not indicate in which accounts wrong entries were made.

100 A

	$	$
Sales		120,000
Opening inventory	2,600	
Purchases	78,900	
Closing inventory	(1,900)	
		(79,600)
Gross profit		40,400
Rental expense (3,400 – 200)	3,200	
Sundry expenses	13,900	
Bank interest	(270)	
Decrease in allowance	(120)	
		(16,710)
Net profit		23,690

101 C

	Dr $	*Cr* $
Premises	500,000	
Provision for depreciation		120,000
Inventory	23,000	
Share capital		200,000
Retained profits		105,000
Receivables	43,500	
Carriage in	1,500	
Allowance for receivables		3,400
Bank overdraft		1,010
Payables		35,900
Sales		500,080
Purchases	359,700	
Sales returns	10,300	
Sundry expenses	14,000	
Discounts allowed	1,340	
Suspense	**12,050**	
	965,390	**965,390**

102 B

	Increase	*Decrease*	
	$	$	
Closing inventory	45,700		
Depreciation (20% × $470,800)		94,160	
Irrecoverable debt		230	
Deferred income		6,700	
	45,700	101,090	
Decrease in net assets			$55,390

103 C

	Charge for the year				Closing
	$				$
Rent	24,000	Rent accrual			**2,000**
		(12 × $2,000)	Due	24,000	
			Paid	22,000	
			Accrual	2,000	
Insurance	28,000	Insurance prepayment			**2,000**
		Paid		30,000	
		Due		28,000	
		Prepayment		2,000	

The rental charge in the income statement will be $24,000 ($2,000 × 12 months). Only $22,000 has been paid, therefore an accrual of $2,000 will appear in the statement of financial position. The insurance charge will be according to the notes given after the trial balance totalling $28,000. The amount paid is $30,000, thus a prepayment of $2,000 will appear in the statement of financial position.

Note: In the trial balance the amount paid will be shown.

104 A

		$
Irrecoverable debts	1,600 + 3,000	4,600
Decrease in allowance for receivables **(W1)**		(440)
Total bad debt expense		4,160
Receivables	(29,600 – 3,000)	26,600
Less:	Closing allowance for receivables	(2,660)
Net closing receivables		23,940

(W1)

Closing allowance for receivables [10% × (26,600 − 3,000)]	2,660
Opening allowance for receivables	3,100
Decrease in allowance for receivables	440

105 B

Depreciation charge	= Closing cost × percentage depreciation rate
	= **$5,000** (10% × $50,000)
Closing accumulated depreciation	= Accumulated depreciation b/f + charge for the year
	= $15,000 + $5,000
	= $20,000
Net book value	= Closing cost less closing accumulated depreciation
Net book value	=$50,000 − $20,000
	= **$30,000**

106 D

Depreciation charge	= (Closing cost − accumulated depreciation b/f) × percentage depreciation rate
	= ($50,000 − $21,875) × 25%
	= $7,031
Closing accumulated depreciation	= Accumulated depreciation b/f + charge for the year
	= £21,875 + £7,031
	= £ 28,906
Net book value	= Closing cost less closing accumulated depreciation
Net book value	= $50,000 − $28,906
Net book value	= $21,094

BOOKS OF PRIME ENTRY AND CONTROL ACCOUNTS

107 C

Day books include:

- Sales day book
- Purchases day book
- Sales returns day book
- Purchases returns day book
- Cash book
- Petty cash book
- The journal

108 B

The imprest amount, or float can always be calculated by adding together the amount in petty cash and the vouchers evidencing expenditure:

\$25 + \$(7.25 + 12.75 + 15) = \$60

109 A

- X = Q = the imprest amount (float).
- Therefore Y (expenses) must be equal to Z (reimbursement).

110 C

Receivables ledger control account

	\$		\$
Balance b/f	69,472		
Sales	697,104	Cash received	686,912
		Irrecoverable debts	1,697
		Sales returns (β)	3,004
		Balance c/f	74,963
	766,576		766,576

111 A

Opening float	150
Receipts	
Photocopier use	25
Bank	500
Payments	
Cheque cashed	(90)
Payments (β)	385
Closing float	200

112 B

A debit balance on a purchase ledger account means that the business is owed money by its supplier. This could be explained by the company mistakenly paying too much. (For example, a business might pay the full amount of an invoice and then receive a 'credit note' from the supplier for the return of faulty goods.)

113 A

Payables ledger control account

	$		$
Bank	68,900	Balance b/f	34,500
Discounts received	1,200	Purchases (credit)	78,400
Purchase returns	4,700		
Balance c/f	38,100		
	112,900		112,900
		Balance b/f	38,100

114 B

Receivables ledger control account

	$		$
Sales	250,000	Bank	225,000
Bank: cheque returned	3,500	Sales returns	2,500
		Irrecoverable debts	3,000
		Contra: trade payables	4,000
		Balance c/f	19,000
	253,500		253,500
Balance b/f	19,000		

115 C

The control account cannot ensure that the personal ledger is free from error. The two totals can agree, but there may be compensating errors in the personal ledger (e.g. the wrong account is debited) or an entry may be missing from both the control account and the ledger.

116 D

A credit entry in the accounts of Y means either that Y owes X $450 or that X owes Y $450 less than before. A credit entry would arise in Y's receivables ledger if customer X returned goods to Y. All the other transactions in the question would result in debit entries.

117 D

The sales day book provides totals for receivables, sales excluding sales tax and tax on the sales. These totals are transferred to the general ledger by debiting the receivables ledger control account with the gross amount receivable, crediting the sales account with the value of sales excluding tax and crediting the sales tax account with the amount of tax payable.

118 B

There is no real point in introducing significant controls to protect an asset worth a maximum of $100 at any given time. Keeping the box locked in a drawer will reduce the risk of it being picked up and stolen without imposing undue inefficiencies or delays in reimbursing valid claims.

119 A

- B describes a purchase order.
- C describes a supplier statement.
- D describes a remittance advice.

120 C

- Quotations are used by a customer to establish the price of goods from various suppliers.
- Goods delivery notes are provided by a supplier to detail goods delivered.
- Debit notes are issued by a customer to cross refer to credit notes issued by a supplier.
- Remittance advice slips are issued by the customer to send to the supplier alongside payment.
- Sales orders are internal documents used by suppliers to record details of orders for goods.
- Purchase orders are sent to suppliers by a customer as a request for supply.
- Purchase invoices are issued by suppliers as a request for payment.

CONTROL ACCOUNT RECONCILIATIONS

121 B

	PLCA		*Payables ledger*
	$		$
Draft balance	768,420	Draft balance	781,200
Reverse incorrect debit entry	28,400		
Discounts received – correct entry	(15,620)		
Revised balance	781,200		781,200

- A and D would explain the discrepancy if the balance on the control account was $12,780 greater than the balance on the payables ledger.
- C would explain the balance on the payables ledger being $25,560 greater than the balance on the control account.

122 A

Payables ledger control account

	$		$
Contras against debit balances in receivables ledger	48,000	Balance b/f	318,600
Cash paid to suppliers	1,364,300	Purchases	1,268,600
Purchase returns	41,200	Refunds received from suppliers	2,700
Discounts received	8,200		
Balance c/f	**128,200**		
	1,589,900		1,589,900

123 D

	Payables ledger	*Supplier statement*
	$	$
Per question	230	3,980
Cheque (1)		(270)
Goods returned (2)		(180)
Contra (3)		(3,200)
Revised balance	230	330

Difference $100 (330 – 230)

124 A

The control account has been debited by $10 more than it should have been. The account should be credited. This error would have had no effect on the receivables ledger and so part of the difference has been explained.

125 B

	Lord's records
	$
Per question	14,500
Unrecorded discount	(150)
Revised balance = supplier statement	14,350

Lord believes that he owes $150 more than the supplier has stated. Items A, C and D would result in the opposite.

126 D

Items A and B will result in an error in the control account. Item C will result in an error in the total of individual customer account balances. Item D will not affect either of the totals, although there are errors in the individual accounts of the two customers affected, with one account balance too high and the other too low by the same amount.

127 D

	SLCA
	$
Draft balance per question	37,642
Correction of misposted discount	(1,802)
Revised balance = receivables ledger balance	35,840

The balance on the control account exceeds the total of the individual account balances by $1,802. Items A, B and C would all have the effect of making the total of the individual account balances higher by $1,802. Item D, however, by recording a credit item as a debit item in the control account, has made the control account debit balance too high by $901 × 2 = $1,802.

128 B

	$
Balance per ledger account	260
Cash discount disallowed	80
Adjusted ledger account balance	340

	$
Balance per supplier's statement	1,350
Less: Goods returned	(270)
Cash in transit	(830)
Revised balance	250

Unreconciled difference = ($340 – $250) = $90

129 D

- The purchase day book has been undercast by $500 (i.e. the total is $500 lower than it should be). As a result of this, the purchases account has been debited and the payables ledger control account (total payables) credited with $500 too little.
- The sales day book has been overcast by $700. As a result, the sales account has been credited and the receivables ledger control account (total receivables) has been debited with $700 too much.
- As a result of these errors, the control account balances need to be adjusted, and profit reduced by ($500 + $700) $1,200, by reducing sales and increasing purchases.
- Neither error affects the entries in the accounts of individual customers and suppliers.

130 A

- As a result of the error, total payables are understated by $259,440 – $254,940 = $4,500. To correct the error, increase the balance in the payables ledger control account by crediting the control account.
- The error has affected the control account only, and not the entries in the individual supplier account for Figgins in the purchase ledger, so the total of suppliers' balances is unaffected.

131 B

Error 1. Total sales and total receivables have been recorded $370 too much. Credit the receivables ledger control account by $370.

Error 2. Total receivables has been recorded ($940 – $490) $450 too little. Credit the receivables ledger control account by $450

As a result of these two errors, total receivables have been under-credited by $820 ($450 + $370).

The errors have not affected the accounts of individual customers.

BANK RECONCILIATIONS

132 D

Cash book	$	
Cash book balance per question	(1,350)	Credit therefore overdrawn
Standing order not yet recorded	(300)	
Revised cash book balance	(1,650)	

	$
Balance per bank statement (β)	(1,707)
Unpresented cheques	(56)
Uncleared lodgements	128
Bank error	(15)
Revised balance = cash book balance	(1,650)

On the bank statement the overdrawn balance is shown as a debit (i.e. from the bank's perspective they are owed money)

133 B

Note that the draft ledger account balance shows an overdraft, however the bank statement shows a positive balance:

	Bank statement	*Ledger account*
	$	$
Balance per question	250	(190)
Unpresented cheques	(150)	
Misposting of cash receipt		260
Bank interest		30
	100	100

134 C

1 Unpresented cheques are those issued by a business but not yet banked by the recipient. They should be deducted from the balance shown on the bank statement in order to reflect the true bank balance.

2 A dishonoured cheque is recorded by crediting the cash book. The cheque would previously have been debited to cash when received. The credit is the reversal of that entry.

3 A bank error should be corrected by amendment to the balance per the bank statement.

4 From the bank's perspective an overdraft means that they are owed money by the customer. Hence it is shown as a debit (an asset to the bank) in the bank statement.

135 B

	$
Balance per bank statement (overdrawn)	(38,640)
Add: Lodgment not credited	19,270
	(19,370)
Less: Unpresented cheques	(14,260)
Balance per cash book	(33,630)

136 B

	$
Balance per bank statement	(200)
Unpresented cheques	(1,250)
Error	97
Uncleared lodgments	890
Revised balance = revised cash book balance	(463)

137 B

	$
Cash book balance	(8,970)
Bank charges	(550)
Revised cash book balance	(9,520)
Bank statement balance (β)	(11,200)
Unpresented cheques	(3,275)
Uncleared lodgements	5,380
Bank error	(425)
Revised cash book balance	(9,520)

138 B

Cash

	$		$
Original balance (β)	11,960		
Error: receipt recorded as payment (2 × $195)	390	Dishonoured cheque	300
		Bank charges	50
		Balance c/f (= revised bank balance)	12,000
	12,350		12,350

	$
Bank statement balance	13,400
Unpresented cheques	(1,400)
Revised balance	12,000

139 D

	$
Balance per bank statement	(715)
Less: Unpresented cheques	(824)
	(1,539)
Add: Outstanding lodgements	337
	(1,202)
Less: Bank error	(25)
Statement of financial position/cash book overdraft	(1,227)

140 D

Cash

	$		$
		Draft balance	5,675
Reversal of standing order (entered twice)	125	Dishonoured cheque	900
Revised balance	6,450		
	6,575		6,575

Note: The dishonoured cheque for $450 should have been credited to the bank balance. Instead it was debited. The bank balance is therefore too high by $900.

141 B

Cash book

	$		$
Cash sales	1,450	Balance b/f	485
Cash receipts	2,400	Payments to suppliers (95% × $1,800)	1,710
		Dishonoured cheques	250
		Balance c/f	1,405
	3,850		3,850

142 B

	$
Balance per bank statement	(800)
Unpresented cheque	(80)
Revised bank balance	(880)

The dishonoured cheque requires adjustment in the cash book. After this adjustment, the cash book balance will equal the revised bank balance.

143 B

Cash

	$		$
Draft balance	2,490		
		Bank charges	50
		Dishonoured cheque	140
		Revised balance	2,300
	2,490		2,490

144 A

Cash

	$		$
		Draft balance	1,240
		Bank charges	75
Revised balance	1,315		
	1,315		1,315

	$
Balance per bank statement (β)	(1,005)
Unpresented cheques	(450)
Uncleared lodgements	140
Revised balance = cash book balance	(1,315)

145 C

An unrecorded difference is a transaction that is reflected in the bank statement but has not yet been entered into the cash book – usually because the accountant is not aware of the transaction until advised by the bank.

Examples include direct debits, standing orders, bank charges, bank interest, dishonoured cheques and direct credits.

Uncleared lodgements and unpresented cheques are examples of timing differences – amounts which have been entered into the cash book but have not yet cleared the bank.

CORRECTION OF ERRORS AND SUSPENSE ACCOUNTS

146 A

Suspense account

	$		$
Imbalance on TB	14,550		
(362,350 – 347,800)			
Disposals (2)	9,000		
Allowance for receivables (3)	2,600	Balance c/f	26,150
	26,150		26,150
Balance b/f	26,150		

The suspense account is only affected where the initial debit and credit were unequal:

1 An incorrect entry into the sales day book means that the subtotal of the day book is wrong and both sides of the double entry have been made for the wrong amount. This does not affect the suspense account.

2 An unequal entry has occurred:

		$
Entry was:	Dr Cash	9,000
	(Cr Suspense	9,000)
To correct:	Dr Suspense	9,000
	Cr Disposals	9,000

(Do not worry about the other journals required to record the disposal – they have not been recorded at all and so do not affect the suspense account.)

3 An unequal entry has occurred:

Entry was:	Dr Irrecoverable debt expense	1,300
	Dr Allowance for receivables	1,300
	(Cr Suspense	2,600)
To correct:	Dr Suspense	2,600
	Cr Allowance for receivables	2,600

147 C

- If the sales day book is undercast, then the debit and credit entries to the accounts are equal (although for the wrong amount).
- Discounts allowed should be debited to the discounts allowed account. The debit entry has simply been made to the wrong account. It is assumed that the credit entry is correct and therefore an equal debit and credit entry have been made.
- The omission of an opening accrual or prepayment will always result in an imbalance on the trial balance.
- The undercasting of the debit side of the cash account will result in an incorrect balance for cash being extracted and shown on the trial balance. This will cause total debit balances to be unequal to total credit balances.

148 A

- An extraction error arises when the balance on a particular account is not listed correctly in the trial balance. Therefore the trial balance does not balance.
- An error of commission arises where an equal debit and credit have been recorded but one entry has been made to the wrong account.
- An error of omission arises where a transaction has been completely omitted from the accounting records.
- An error of original entry arises where an equal debit and credit have been made but for the wrong amount.

149 D

- The suspense account initially has a credit balance in order to make the total debits equal to the total credits.
- Where an opening accrual has been omitted, it should be recorded and the opposite entry made to the suspense account:

Dr Suspense account	$7,568
Cr Rental expense	$7,568

Suspense account

	$		$
Opening accrual	7,568	Per trial balance	7,568

Tutorial note:

Discounts allowed should be a debit in the trial balance of $3,784. If the account balance is wrongly shown as a credit, the total credits in the trial balance will exceed the total debits by 2 × $3,784.

Discounts received

Correct entry		*Actual entry*	
Dr Payables ledger control account	$3,784	Cr Payables ledger control account	$3,784
Cr Discounts received.	$3,784	Cr Discounts received	$3,784
		(Dr Suspense account	$7,568

The actual entry made was a double credit. This will result in a debit balance arising on the suspense account.

Sales day book

If the sales day book is undercast, the entries to the sales and receivables ledger control accounts will be equal, but for the wrong amount. This will not result in an imbalance on the trial balance.

150 C

- The correct entry for discounts allowed is:

Dr Discounts allowed

Cr Receivables ledger control account (receivables)

- As the debit was made to the discounts received account in error, the amount needs reversing out of the discounts received account by way of a credit.
- The correct debit should then be posted to the discounts allowed account.

Note:

- Personal accounts are not maintained for the directors of a company
- Where repairs are carried out by a company's own staff using items of inventory , the correct journal to transfer the relevant costs to the repairs account is:

Dr Repairs

Cr Wages/purchases

If rent received is credited to the wrong account, no suspense account entry arises. The correction journal will involve debiting the account wrongly credited and crediting the rent receivable account.

151 B

1 A debit and credit are made for an equal amount (albeit to the wrong account in the case of the debit), and therefore the suspense account is not affected.

2 The undercasting of the debit side of the wages account will result in an incorrect balance being extracted. This will result in an imbalance on the trial balance and the creation of a suspense account.

3 The correct entry for discounts allowed is:

Dr Discounts allowed

Cr Receivables ledger control account (receivables)

The error made will therefore result in a double credit (correctly to the receivables ledger control account, and incorrectly to discounts received). Where double entry breaks down, a suspense account will be created.

4 An equal debit and credit entry are made and therefore the suspense account is not affected.

152 C

Should do		*Did do*		*To correct*	
Dr Discounts allowed	13,000	Cr Discounts received	13,000	Dr Discounts received	13,000
Cr SLCA (receivables)	13,000	Cr SLCA (receivables)	13,000	Dr Discounts allowed	13,000
		(Dr Suspense	26,000)	Cr Suspense	13,000
Dr Plant and machinery	18,000	(Dr Suspense	18,000)	Dr Plant and machinery	18,000
Cr Cash	18,000	Cr Cash	18,000	Cr Suspense	18,000

153 B

1 Double entry has been maintained (an equal debit and credit entry have been made). Therefore there is no effect on the suspense account.

To correct:	Dr Plant account	$43,200
	Cr Cash	$43,200

In addition, depreciation should have been charged at 10% × $48,000, i.e. $4,800.

To record extra depreciation:	Dr Depreciation expense	$4,320
	Cr Accumulated depreciation	$4,320

2 This transaction has been omitted completely from the accounts therefore it has no effect on the suspense account.

To correct:	Dr Bank charges	$440
	Cr Cash	$440

3 A debit entry has been made, but no credit entry. A suspense account entry will therefore be required to correct this error:

Should do		*Did do*		*To correct*	
Dr Payables ledger account	$800	Dr Payables ledger account	$800	Dr Suspense	$800
Cr Sundry payables (amount due to Director)	$800	(Cr suspense	$800)	Cr Sundry payables	$800

4 The balance on the cash book will be $10,000 too high as a result of the understatement. Therefore the trial balance will not balance and a suspense account will arise.

To correct:	Dr Suspense	$10,000
	Cr Cash	$10,000

154 D

Correction journals only affect profit if one side is posted to an income statement account and the other to a statement of financial position account. For this purpose, a suspense account is a statement of financial position account:

		Increase	*Decrease*	
		$	$	$
Draft profit				630,000
1	Extra depreciation		4,320	
2	Bank charges		440	
3	No effect			
4	No effect			
				(4,760)
				625,240

155 C

Profit is only affected when one (but not both) side of the correction journal is posted to the income statement.

- Both entries in the journal to record cash drawings are to statement of financial position accounts.
- The expense of $420 has already been recorded when the allowance was made during the year.
- To correct the misclassification, interest receivable will be reduced and rental income increased by the same amount. Therefore there is no effect on profit.
- Both entries in the journal to record the receipt are to statement of financial position accounts.

156 C

Should do		*Did do*		*To correct*	
Dr Purchases	$4,000	Dr Purchases	$4,700	Dr Suspense	$700
Dr Sales tax	$700	Dr Sales tax	$700	Cr Purchases	$700
Cr PLCA	$4,700	Cr PLCA	$4,700		
		(Cr Suspense	$700)		

- Purchases (and sales) are recorded net of sales tax.
- Payables (and receivables) are recorded gross of sales tax.

157 A

Suspense account

	$		$
Balance per TB	500	Misrecording of decrease in allowance for receivables	840
Sales account undercast	150		
Balance c/f	190		–
	840		840
		Balance b/f	190

- The misposting of rent received to the rent payable account does not affect the suspense account as double entry was maintained, despite the error.

158 C

An error of principle breaks the 'rules' of an accounting principle or concept, for example incorrectly treating revenue expenditure as capital expenditure. The purchase of a non-current asset should be debited to a non-current asset account, not to the purchases account.

159 B

Should do		*Did do*		*To correct*	
1 Dr Motor expense	$4,600	Cr Cash	$4,600	Dr Motor expense	$4,600
Cr Cash	$4,600	Cr MV cost	$4,600	Dr MV cost	$4,600
		(Dr Suspense	$9,200)	Cr Suspense	$9,200
2 Dr Cash	$360	Dr Cash	$360	Dr Green's account	$360
Cr Brown's account	$360	Cr Green's account	$360	Cr Brown's account	$360
3 Dr Rent expense	$9,500	Dr Rent expense	$5,900	Dr Rent expense	$3,600
Cr Cash	$9,500	Cr Cash	$9,500	Cr Suspense	$3,600
		(Dr Suspense	$3,600)		
4 Dr Discounts allowed		Dr Discounts received		Dr Discounts allowed	
Cr SLCA		Cr SLCA		Cr Discounts received	
5 Dr Cash	$100	–		Dr Cash	$100
Cr Sales	$100			Cr Sales	$100

160 B

By crediting $40 to the Discounts Allowed account, when the discount should have been debited to the account, discounts allowed have been reduced by $40 when they should have been increased by $40. As a result of this error, profit has been overstated by 2 × $40 = $80.

161 A

Should do	*Did do*	*To correct*
1 Dr Gas expense $420	Dr Gas expense $240	Dr Gas expense $180
Cr Cash $420	Cr Cash $420	Cr Suspense $180
	(Dr Suspense $180)	
2 Dr Discounts allowed $50	Cr Discounts received $50	Dr Discounts allowed $50
Cr SLCA $50	Cr SLCA $50	Dr Discounts received $50
	(Dr Suspense $100)	Cr Suspense $100
3 Dr Bank $70	Dr Bank $70	Dr Suspense $70
Cr Interest $70	(Cr Suspense $70)	Cr Interest $70

Suspense account

	$		$
Balance b/f (β)	210	Error 1	180
Error 3	70	Error 2	100
	280		280

162 D

The error has been to debit the customer (receivable) account and credit the supplier (payable) account, instead of debiting the supplier account and crediting the customer account. As a result receivables are over-stated by 2 × $270 = $540, and payables are over-stated by $540. The error should be corrected, but sales and purchases are unaffected, so profit is unaffected. Total assets (receivables) and total liabilities (payables) are both $540 too high, so that net assets are unchanged.

APPLICATIONS OF INFORMATION TECHNOLOGY

163 C

- Computer systems tend to be less flexible than manual systems because of the detailed work required in maintaining and developing programs. Maintenance and development is also costly and takes a long time.
- The computer is a machine and therefore it cannot pick up errors or incomplete data that a clerk in a manual system may notice.

164 B

- A manual system can hold as much information as a database; the advantage of a database in this respect is that it takes up less space.

165 A

- A computerised system will be broken down into sections in the same way as a manual system; each will be accessible only to authorised personnel.
- A computerised general ledger tends to be a listing of debits and credits rather, not a collection of T accounts. Double entry is still, however, being performed.

166 B

167 A

- Goal seeking facility is the ability of a spreadsheet, when given an output value, to produce all possible combinations of input value.
- Flexibility is provided in terms of inserting and deleting columns and rows in a spreadsheet and moving sections of text around the spreadsheet.
- Look up tables are values held in a table which can be selected for insertion in specific cells.
- 'What if' analysis is the ability of a spreadsheet to complete sensitivity analysis, i.e. assess the effect of one piece of data changing value on the remaining data.
- Many spreadsheets can use the data contained within them to produce graphs and charts.

INCOMPLETE RECORDS

168 A

	$	$	%
Sales		650,000	100
Cost of sales			
Opening inventory	380,000		
Purchases	480,000		
Lost inventory (β)	**(185,000)**		
Closing inventory	(220,000)		
		(455,000)	70
Gross profit		195,000	30

169 D

	$	$	%
Sales (100/70 × $756,000)		**1,080,000**	100
Cost of sales			
Opening Inventory	77,000		
Purchases	763,000		
Closing Inventory	(84,000)		
		(756,000)	70
		324,000	30

170 B

	$	$	%
Sales (174,825 – 1,146)		173,679	125%
Cost of goods sold			
Opening inventory	12,274		
Purchases (136,527 – 1,084)	135,443		
Closing inventory (β)	**(8,774)**		
$173,679 × 100/125		(138,943)	100%
Gross profit		34,736	25%

171 D

	$	$	%
Sales		630,000	140
Cost of sales			
Opening Inventory	24,300		
Purchases (β)	458,450		
Closing Inventory	(32,750)		
100/140 × $630,000		(450,000)	100
		180,000	40

Payables ledger control account

	$		$
		Balance b/f	29,780
Cash paid to suppliers (β)	**453,630**	Purchases (cash and credit)	458,450
Balance c/f	34,600		
	488,230		488,230

172 C

	$
Inventory at 6 January 20X6	32,780
Sales at cost (β)	6,020
Purchases	(4,200)
Inventory at 31 December 20X5	34,600

Profit on sales: $8,600 – $6,020 = $2,580

Gross margin: $\frac{2{,}580}{8{,}600}$ = 30%

173 D

Cash

	$		$
Balance b/f	620		
Receipts from customers (β)	16,660	Payments	16,780
		Balance c/f	500
	17,280		17,280

Receivables

	$		$
Balance b/f	6,340		
Sales (β)	15,520	Cash receipts	16,660
		Balance c/f	5,200
	21,860		21,860

Gross profit: 25/125 × $15,520 = $3,104

174 B

	$	$
Sales		148,000
Opening inventory	34,000	
Purchases	100,000	
	134,000	
Closing inventory (β)	**(26,000)**	
Cost of sales (148,000 – 40,000)		108,000
Gross profit		40,000

175 C

You might need to answer this by testing each answer in turn.

$$\frac{\text{Gross profit}}{\text{Cost of sales}} \qquad \frac{28,800}{72,000} = 40\%$$

	$
Sales	100,800
Cost of sales	(72,000)
Gross profit	28,800

176 D

Trade payables

	$		$
Cash paid	542,300	Balance b/f	142,600
Discounts received	13,200		
Goods returned	27,500		
Balance c/f	137,800	Purchases (β)	**578,200**
	720,800		720,800

177 D

Trade receivables

	$		$
Balance b/f	10,000	Receipts from sales	85,000
Sales (β)	**84,000**		
		Balance c/f	9,000
	94,000		94,000

178 C

Cash

	$		$
Balance b/f	300	Bankings	50,000
Proceeds of sale of car	5,000	Wages	12,000
Sales (β)	**81,100**	Drawings	24,000
		Balance c/f	400
	86,400		86,400

179 C

	$	$	%
Sales		480,000	150
Cost of sales			
Opening inventory	36,420		
Purchases (β)	324,260		
Closing inventory	(40,680)		
100/150 × $480,000		(320,000)	100
		180,000	50

PLCA

	$		$
		Balance b/f	29,590
Cash paid (β)	**319,975**	Purchases	324,260
Balance c/f	33,875		
	353,850		353,850

180 B

Closing net assets	=	Opening net assets	+	Capital injections	–	Loss for the period	–	Drawings
($56,000 – $18,750)		($40,000 – $14,600)						($6,800 + $250)
$37,250	=	$25,400	+	$20,000	–	(β) **$1,100**	–	$7,050

181 D

- As the inventory is insured, its cost (not selling price) is recoverable from the insurer. Therefore this amount is shown as a current asset.
- The cost should also be taken out of cost of sales as these goods have not been sold.

PARTNERSHIP ACCOUNTS

182 D

Karen – current account

	$		$
		Balance b/f	X
Drawings	20,000	Salary	**25,000**
		Profit share	**58,125**
		3/8 (180,000 – 25,000)	
Balance c/f	63,125		
	83,125		83,125

183 A

Current account – Julian

	$		$
Balance b/f	13,000	Interest on capital	4,750
		5% × $95,000	
Drawings (cash)	34,000	Profit share (W)	117,375
Drawings (tax)	12,400		
Balance c/f	62,725		
	122,125		122,125
		Balance b/f	**62,725**

(W) Profit share

	$
Profit	250,000
Interest on capital 5% ($100,000 + $110,000 + $95,000)	(15,250)
Profit to be shared in ratio 1:2:3	234,750
Julian's share: 3/6 × $234,750	117,375

184 C

- Interest is sometimes charged to partners who withdraw cash from the business before the end of the financial year.
- Where this is the case, the amount charged will increase the profit available to share between the partners in the profit share ratio.

185 C

	Jeremy	*Nicky*	*Total*
	$	$	$
6 months ended 30 June X6			
Salary (6/12 × $40,000)	20,000		20,000
Interest on capital			
$200,000 × 5% × 6/12	5,000	2,500	7,500
$100,000 × 5% × 6/12			
PSR 1:1	70,625	70,625	(β) 141,250
Profits $337,500 × 6/12			168,750
6 months ended 31 December X6			
Interest on capital			
$200,000 × 5% × 6/12	5,000	5,000	10,000
PSR 1: 1	79,375	79,375	(β) 158,750
Profits $337,500 × 6/12			168,750
Total	**180,000**	157,500	337,500

186 D

	Albus	*Brio*	*Corbin*	*Total*
	$	$	$	$
Six months ended 31.12.X5				
PSR 3:2	180,000	120,000		300,000
Six months ended 30.6.X6				
Irrecoverable debt				
3/5 × $50,000 / 2/5 × $50,000	(30,000)	(20,000)		(50,000)
PSR 4:3:3	200,000	150,000	150,000	(β) 500,000
				450,000
Total	**350,000**	250,000	150,000	

187 C

Partners are jointly and severally liable for the losses of the partnership, i.e. each partner is potentially liable for a full loss regardless of which partner's actions resulted in that loss.

188 B

A partnership agreement includes 'standing information' such as:

- The name and type of business.
- Capital introduced by partners.
- Details of profit share arrangements.
- Details of drawings.
- Arrangements for the dissolution of the partnership, or on the death or retirement of partners.
- Settling of disputes.
- Preparation and audit of accounts.

It does not tend to include operational details such as a list of approved suppliers.

189 C

	Lewis	*Hamilton*	*Total*
	$	$	$
Salary	12,000	–	12,000
Interest on capital 3% × $10,000 / $20,000			
	300	600	900
PSR 1:4	370	1,480	1,850 (β)
			14,750
	12,670	**2,080**	

190 D

	Woody	*Buzz*	*Total*
	$	$	$
Salary	9,000	12,000	21,000
Interest on capital 10% × $30,000 / $15,000			
	3,000	1,500	4,500
Interest on drawings 5% × $4,000 × 3/12			
	(50)		(50)
PSR 1:4	(40,725)	(40,725)	(81,450) (β)
			(56,000)
	(28,775)	(27,225)	

191 C

	Pat	*Ajay*	*Meera*	*Total*
	$	$	$	$
Salary	–	16,000	–	16,000
Interest on capital				
4% × $14,000	560			
4% × $10,000 × 6/12		200		1,380
4% × $15,000 × 6/12		300		
4% × $8,000			320	
Profit share (5:3:2)	12,310	7,386	4,924	24,620 (β)
				42,000
Total	12,870	23,886	5,244	
Adjustment	(472.50)	(283.5)	756	
Revised total	12,397.50	**23,602.50**	6,000	

192 B

Revised profit after loan interest $75,993 ($76,393 – 400)

	Fleurie	*Beaune*	*Argento*	*Total*
	$	$	$	$
Salary	15,000	15,000	–	30,000
Interest on capital				
6% × $18,000/$20,000/$30,000	1,080	1,200	1,800	4,080
PSR 3:2:4	13,971	9,314	18,628	41,913 (β)
Total	30,051	25,514	20,428	75,993

Current account – Beaune

	$		$
Balance b/f	10,000	Share of profits	25,514
		Loan interest outstanding	400
		8% × $20,000 × 3/12	
Balance c/f	15,914		
	25,914		25,914
		Balance b/f	**15,914**

193 C

Capital account – Orla

	$		$
		Balance per question	50,000
Goodwill split in new ratio		Goodwill split in old ratio	
4/15 × $30,000	8,000	3/10 × $30,000	9,000
Balance c/f	51,000		
	59,000		59,000
		Balance b/f	**51,000**

Current accounts are not affected by accounting for goodwill on the admission of a new partner.

194 A

If no goodwill account is maintained, the capital accounts of the partners are debited with the goodwill split in the new ratio and credited with the goodwill split in the old ratio:

Dr Macy capital account (1/9 × $63,000)	$7,000
Dr Bloomingdale capital account (3/9 × $63,000)	$21,000
Dr Saks capital account (5/9 × $63,000)	$35,000
Cr Macy capital account (2/7 × $63,000)	$18,000
Cr Bloomingdale capital account (1/7 × $63,000)	$9,000
Cr Saks capital account (4/7 × $63,000)	$36,000

The net effect on Bloomingdale's capital account is therefore a debit of $12,000.

195 C

Odd – capital account

	$		$
		Balance b/f	45,000
		Revaluation (2/5 × $35,000)	14,000
		Goodwill (2/5 × $40,000)	16,000
Balance c/f	75,000		
	75,000		75,000
		Balance b/f	75,000

196 A

- Partnership goodwill can be calculated in a number of different ways, one of which is to attribute a value based on a multiple of profit.
- Goodwill is considered when a partner joins or leaves the business and also when the partners change their profit ratio.

197 B

Ami is entitled to $21,000. She only received $18,000. The shortfall/deficit is therefore $3,000.

This deficit has to be shared between the remaining two partners in their remaining profit share ratio.

Kami and Shati will share the shortfall/deficit in the ratio of 2:3.

Kami's share $2/5 \times \$3,000$ =	$1,200
Shati's share $3/5 \times \$3,000$ =	$1,800

After the adjustment for the guaranteed minimum share, the following will be the profit share:

Ami	$21,000
Kami ($20,000 – $1,200)	$18,200
Shati ($25,000 – $1,800)	$23,200

COMPANY ACCOUNTS

198 C

	Cost of sales	*Administrative expense*	*Distribution costs*
	$	$	$
Opening inventory	12,500		
Closing inventory	(17,900)		
Purchases	199,000		
Distribution costs			35,600
Administrative expenses		78,800	
Audit fee		15,200	
Carriage in	3,500		
Carriage out			7,700
Depreciation (70:30:0)	28,000	12,000	
	225,100	106,000	43,300

199 B

- The first statement is false: the nominal value of the ordinary shares is 50c and therefore there are 200,000 in issue. The ordinary dividend paid is:

  $200,000 \times 3c = \$6,000$

- The second statement is true. A preference dividend is accounted for when it falls due and therefore the part of the dividend not yet paid must be accrued at the year end.

200 C

Share premium

	$		$
		Balance b/f	30,000
Bonus issue (W2)	12,500	Rights issue (W1)	90,000
Balance c/f	107,500		
	120,000		120,000

(W1)	**Rights issue**	Existing number of shares	400,000
		New shares	100,000
	At $1.15 each	Dr Cash	$115,000
		Cr Share capital	$25,000
		Cr Share premium	$90,000
(W2)	**Bonus issue**	Existing shares	500,000
		New shares	50,000
		Dr Share premium	$12,500
		Cr Share capital	$12,500

201 D

- Only dividend income is shown in the statement of comprehensive income.
- Only dividends payable in respect of preference shares are shown in the statement of financial position.
- The statement of cash flows includes all dividends paid.
- The statement of changes in equity includes dividends paid and dividends payable.

202 C

- The tax charge is disclosed in the statement of comprehensive income.
- A revaluation surplus is not realised. However, under IAS 1 (revised) it is included in the statement of comprehensive income and also shown in the statement of changes in equity.

203 D

- Dividends are not shown in a company's statement of comprehensive income. Instead they are presented in the statement of changes to equity.
- Unpaid ordinary dividends are only accrued at the year end if they have been declared prior to the year end. In practise this is very rare.

204 A

- A rights issue involves the issue of new shares for cash and therefore more equity capital will be raised.
- The rights issue price will probably be above nominal value and therefore the share premium account will be increased by the amount of the premium. A bonus issue does not involve cash; when recording the transaction, the debit entry is normally made to the share premium account, therefore reducing it.
- Both a rights and a bonus issue involve the potential issue of shares to existing shareholders. Therefore neither will increase the number of shareholders in a company.
- A bonus issue will result in more shares in issue without affecting the value of the company as a whole. Therefore each share will be worth less, not more.

205 C

- An overprovision from a previous year reduces the tax charge to the statement of comprehensive income.
- Tax payable is the full amount of the estimation of the charge for the year.

206 C

- The credit sale is part of the company's normal operating cycle and is therefore classified as a current asset.
- The bank overdraft is repayable on demand and so classified as a current liability.
- The shares have been purchased to sell and so are classified as a current asset investment.

207 D

	Share capital	*Share premium*	*Revaluation reserve*	*Retained earnings*	*Total*
	$	$	$	$	$
Share issue	2,000	3,000			5,000
Revaluation			230,000		230,000
Net profit					
(178,000 – 45,000 – 5,600)				127,400	127,400
Dividends – ordinary				(12,000)	(12,000)
– preference				(8,000)	(8,000)
Total change	2,000	3,000	230,000	107,400	342,400

208 D

- Preference shares do not generally carry voting rights.
- Preference dividends are fixed amounts, normally expressed as a percentage of their nominal value.
- Preference dividends are paid out in preference to ordinary dividends.

209 A

- Accounting standards require that the commercial substance of a transaction is recorded rather than its legal form.
- Redeemable preference shares are repayable at a specified future date and therefore have the qualities of debt.
- They are therefore accounted for as liabilities.

210 B

- Paid up share capital is the amount of the nominal value which have been paid currently.
- Issued share capital is the share capital which has actually been issued to shareholders.
- Authorised share capital is the nominal value of the maximum number of shares that a company can have in issue at any one time.

211 B

- Loan notes can be issued at a discount to their nominal value (unlike shares).
- Interest is always paid based on the nominal value.
- Interest accrued \$8,000 (12% × \$400,000 × 2/12)

212 A

- A bonus share issue does not raise finance for a company, as the shares are issued for no consideration (i.e. for free).
- Each share becomes worth less (as there are more shares in issue but the value of the company as a whole remains the same), and so more marketable.
- The reserves decreases when there is a bonus issue. The double entry is to debit the reserves and credit the share capital.
- Share capital increases (at the expense of other reserves) and so may seem more appropriate when compared to net assets.

213 B

The share premium and revaluation reserves are **capital reserves**, however the accumulated profits and general reserves are **revenue** reserves.

ACCOUNTING STANDARDS

214 C

- A flood does not provide additional information to conditions existing at the year end and therefore is non-adjusting.
- The credit customer's bankruptcy occurs after the accounts are approved.
- The declaration of an ordinary dividend is a non-adjusting event.

215 A

- The refund policy creates a constructive obligation.
- Provision should be made for the best estimate of the value of refunds. This may be based on expected values.
- The legal claim is only possible, therefore the company can not provide for the loss; instead they should disclose details of the case.

216 B

The right will generate future economic benefits, so it is an asset. It will be retained and used in the business and will not turn itself directly into cash in the normal course of business, so it is not a current asset. It has no physical existence, so it is an intangible non-current asset.

217 A

- Intangible assets may be internally generated or purchased.
- They are often used to generate profits in the long term.
- Their key characteristic is their lack of physical substance.

218 A

219 D

- Details of adjusting events are not disclosed by note; instead the event is accounted for.
- The sale of inventory after the reporting date at a price lower than that at which it is valued in the statement of financial position is an adjusting event.
- A fall in the market value of investments after the reporting date is a non-adjusting event. It should therefore be disclosed if material.

220 A

- Warranties meet the criteria required to create a provision; a provision should be made for the best estimate of the obligation.
- The likelihood of a liability arising for Quidditch as a result of the guarantee is assessed as possible. A provision can not be recorded unless the likelihood is probable.

221 C

The costs of a development project are capitalised only if:

- The project is separately identifiable.
- Expenditure can be reliably measured.
- It is commercially viable.
- It is technically feasible.
- It is projected to be profitable.
- Resources are available to complete it.

- Project 2 falls short of these criteria: it does not appear that the appetite suppressant properties of the substance have yet been confirmed and therefore it is not yet commercially viable.
- Project 3 may not be completed and therefore does not meet all six criteria.
- The costs of projects 2 and 3 should be expensed to the statement of comprehensive income.

222 A

	$
Project A	34,000
Project B	78,870
Project C ($290,000 + $19,800) × 4/36	34,422
	147,292

- Project A is a research project and all costs should be written off to the statement of comprehensive income as incurred.
- Project B is a development project. Costs can only be capitalised once the capitalisation criteria are met. Those costs incurred before this was the case cannot be reinstated as an asset.
- Project C is a development project which has resulted in capitalised expenditure. This asset must be amortised over the 36 months of sales of the product. Amortisation for the current year should be 4 months (1 September to 31 December 20X5).

223 B

- 1 is a change in accounting estimate and should be accounted for prospectively (i.e. the change should be applied going forward, but previous periods' figures should not be revised).
- 2 is a change in accounting policy and should be accounted for retrospectively (i.e. opening reserves are adjusted to show the position as if the new policy had always been in place).

224 B

- Revenue should not be recognised on the first transaction until the specialist installation is complete.
- The second transaction is a normal credit sale and revenue should be recognised regardless of the fact that cash has not yet been received.

225 D

The conditions which must be satisfied in order to record revenue from the sale of goods are:

- Revenue can be measured reliably.
- Benefits are likely to flow to the entity.
- The stage of completion of the service can be reliably measured.
- Costs incurred for the transaction can be measured reliably.

STATEMENT OF CASH FLOWS

226 D

	$
Issue of shares (560,000 – 220,000)	340,000
Issue of loan notes	300,000
	640,000

- Interest paid is included within the 'operating activities' heading of the cash flow statement.

227 B

- Interest received = $13,000.
- Interest and dividends paid are normally shown within cash from operating activities. An alternative presentation may place them within cash from financing activities.

228 C

- Bonus issues do not involve the transfer of cash, whereas rights issues result in a cash inflow.
- The revaluation of non-current assets does not involve the transfer of cash.

229 D

- Depreciation is a non-cash expense and should therefore be added back to profit.
- An increase in assets (inventory and receivables) means that less cash is available (as it has been used to fund assets), hence an increase in assets is shown as a deduction in the cash flow statement.
- An increase in liabilities (payables) means that more cash is available (i.e. it has not been used to pay liabilities), hence an increase in liabilities is shown as an addition in the cash flow statement.

230 D

- The carrying value off non-current assets is shown in the statement of financial position.
- Depreciation charged on non-current assets and any profit or loss on disposal is shown in the statement of comprehensive income.
- Revaluation surpluses relating to non-current assets are shown in the statement of changes in equity.
- In relation to non-current assets, the indirect statement of cash flows will include:
  - depreciation
  - profit or loss on disposal
  - proceeds of the disposal of non-current assets
  - payments to acquire non-current assets.

231 D

	$	
Cash generated from operations (β)	419,254	
Tax and dividends paid	(87,566)	
Net cash from operating activities (β)		331,688
Purchase of property, plant and equipment	(47,999)	
Proceeds from sale of property, plant and equipment	13,100	
Net cash from investing activities		(34,899)
Redemption of loans	(300,000)	
Net cash from financing activities		(300,000)
Decrease in cash and cash equivalents		(3,211)

232 A

	$000
Profit for the year (β)	**1,175**
Add back depreciation	100
Less: Increase in receivables & inventory	(575)
Cash flow from operating activities	700
Add: Cash from issue of shares	1,000
Less: Repayment of debentures	(750)
Less: Purchase of non-current assets	(200)
Increase in cash	750

233 B

Non-current assets book value

	$		$
Balance b/f	50,000	Disposals (4,000 – 1,500)	2,500
Additions (β)	7,500	Depreciation	9,000
		Balance c//f	46,000
	57,500		57,500

234 C

	$
Profit	8,000
Add: Depreciation (not a cash expense)	12,000
	20,000
Purchase of new non-current assets	(25,000)
Fall in cash balance	(5,000)

235 D

	$000
Profit for the year	18,750
Depreciation	1,250
Non-current asset purchases	(8,000)
Decrease in inventories	1,800
Increase in receivables	(1,000)
Increase in payables	350
Increase in cash and cash equivalents	13,150

236 D

Items added include the depreciation charge for the period, any losses on disposals of non-current assets, reductions in inventories and receivables (including prepayments) and any increase in trade payables (including accruals).

237 D

Statement 1 is incorrect: net cash flow from operating activities is the same, whichever method of presentation is used.

Statement 2 is incorrect. Companies with high profits can be cash-negative, due to high spending on new non-current assets and/or a large build-up of working capital.

Statement 3 is incorrect. Profits and losses on non-current asset disposals are shown as an adjustment to net profit before tax.

238 D

- New purchase (additions) are given in the question as $2,000.
- The assets disposed of had a cost of $3,000 and accumulated depreciation at the time of disposal of $1,500. Their net book value at disposal was therefore $1,500. The profit on disposal was $500, so the cash received from the disposal was $2,000.

239 A

Major non-cash transactions are not highlighted within the statement of cash flows (although they are disclosed elsewhere in a set of accounts). These are of interest to the users of accounts as they may have an impact on future cash flows.

240 D

	$
Cash sales	212,500
Less:	
Cash purchases	(4,600)
Cash expenses	(11,200)
Cash paid to credit suppliers (W1)	(121,780)
Cash paid as wages and salaries (W2)	(33,800)
Cash generated from operations	41,120

(W1)

Payables

	$		$
		Balance b/f	12,300
Cash paid **(β)**	121,780	Purchases	123,780
Balance c/f	14,300		
	136,080		136,080

(W2)

Wages and salaries

	$		$
		Balance b/f	1,500
Cash paid **(β)**	33,800	Statement of comprehensive income expense	34,600
Balance c/f	2,300		
	36,100		36,100

241 C

	$000
Retained profit for the year ($82,000 – $72,000)	10,000
Add back:	
Dividends payable (current year's)	1,600
Tax payable (current year's estimate)	15,000
Loan note interest payable (10% × $40,000)	4,000
Operating profit	30,600

The additional $10,000 loan notes were issued at the beginning of the year. Therefore, the total loan notes at the start of the year will be $40,000. The loan notes interest for the year will be $4,000 (i.e. 10% × $40,000).

REGULATORY FRAMEWORK

242 C

The IFRIC (International Financial Reporting Interpretations Committee) are responsible for providing guidance on emerging issues.

243 C

244 A

Accounting standards provide guidance on common transactions. They cannot provide guidance on all types of transactions.

245 D

- Prudence requires a cautious approach to be taken: gains should not be recorded until realised whereas losses should be recorded when anticipated. This will not result in understated assets or overstated liabilities.
- Commercial substance should always be reflected in financial statements, even where this differs from legal form.
- A revaluation surplus is not realised however, it is credited the statement of comprehensive income and then shown in the statement of changes in equity.

246 A

247 D

The replacement cost of an asset is often referred to as its current cost.

248 D

If a business is a going concern, it is reasonable to assume that non-current assets will be used over their expected useful economic life. It is therefore appropriate to value a non-current asset at cost less accumulated depreciation, which represents the consumption of value so far.

249 B

If the net realisable value (NRV) of inventory is less than its cost then the company then the company has incurred a loss. Writing the inventory down to its net realisable value as soon as that loss has been identified reflects prudence.

250 D

Information that is reliable may take longer to obtain and verify. For example, knowing for certain how much a piece of inventory will sell for requires waiting until it has been sold. Reliable measures are also likely to be based on historical measures that are less appropriate for future oriented decisions. For example, the most reliable measure that can be provided for a piece of equipment is its original cost, which may be quite useless for decision making. More relevant information will frequently require estimates and forecasts to determine.

251 A

Consistency means using the same accounting policies from one year to the next. It is one aspect of comparability (making the financial statements of a business comparable from one year to the next, the other aspect being to make the financial statements of different businesses comparable with one another). Asset valuations and profit measurements are made the same way each year, and this makes it easier to compare the financial position and performance of the business between one year and the next.

252 B

The historical cost concept is to value assets and liabilities at their original cost to the business, and so fails to take account of changing price levels over time. This is a particular problem with assets that are held for a long time and tend to rise in value, particularly land and buildings. However, the historical cost concept does have regard to depreciation of non-current assets and loss in value, so answer C is incorrect.

253 D

Falling prices (deflation) are not usual. If deflation does occur, historical cost accounting will overstate the current value of assets in the statement of financial position. Profits will be understated. Perhaps the easiest way to think about this is that if assets are valued at historical cost when their current value is much lower due to deflation, depreciation charges will be higher and profit lower.

254 C

255 B

The Framework is not an accounting standard itself, although it is used as a basis when new standards are produced.

256 A

- Historical cost accounting maintains financial capital but not physical capital.
- It does not result in the statement of financial position giving an accurate valuation of the business.

Section 3

OBJECTIVE TEST QUESTIONS

1 **A / an ---------- is a resource controlled by the entity as a result of past events and from which future economic benefits are expected to flow to the entity.**

Fill in the blank with a single word typed in lower case **(1 mark)**

2 **The accounting equation can be written as:**

Assets – liabilities – opening capital + ____________ = profit.

Fill in the blank with a single word typed in lower case **(1 mark)**

3 **Payables, tax, loans and overdrafts are all examples of ____________.**

Fill in the blank with a single word typed in lower case **(1 mark)**

4 **A sole trader takes out a loan of $10,000 from the bank. The two elements of the accounting equation that will change as a result of this transaction are assets and ________________.**

Fill in the blank with a single word typed in lower case **(1 mark)**

5 **A sole trader increases the business's number of motor vehicles by adding his own car to its fleet. The two elements of the accounting equation that will change as a result of this transaction are assets and ________________**

Fill in the blank with a single word typed in lower case **(1 mark)**

6 **A sole trader had receivables of $5,400 at 1 September. During May the business made credit sales of $33,000 and received $24,700 from customers. The balance on the receivables account at the end of September was $_______.**

Enter a whole number **WITHOUT** the $ sign **(2 marks)**

7 **A sole trader, in his first month of trading, enters into the following transactions:**

Buys goods for cash for $960

Makes a credit sale to a customer for $500. The customer pays 5 weeks later.

Draws $62 for personal living expenses

Sells goods for cash for £125

The total entry to the debit side of the cash T-account is $____________. **(2 marks)**

8 **Hodgetts Ltd has opening trade payables of $28,682 and closing trade payables of $34,855. Purchases for the period totalled $254,192 with $31,590 relating to cash purchases.**

Total payments recorded in the payables ledger for the period were $__________.

Enter a whole number **WITHOUT** the $ sign **(2 marks)**

9 **Wilson Ltd gives all their customers that buy goods on credit a discount for prompt payment. This is known as a discount __________.**

Fill in the missing word, in lower case **(2 marks)**

10 **Frith had $8,200 of capital invested in his business at the start of the year. During the year he took $150 per month out of the business to cover his personal living expenses. The business' profit for the year was $4,820.**

The balance on the capital account at the year end is $__________.

Enter a whole number WITHOUT the $ sign **(2 marks)**

11 **Amelia values her inventory using AVCO. At 1 March 20X9 there were 60 units in inventory valued at $12 each. On 12 March, 40 units were purchased for $15 each and on the 18 March a further 50 units were purchased for $18 each. On the 30 March, 70 units were sold for $20 each.**

The value of closing inventory at 31 March 20X9 was $__________.

Enter a whole number WITHOUT the $ sign **(2 marks)**

12 **Taylor has two products in inventory at the year end, 6000 units of product A and 2000 units of product B.**

The following information is available:

All 6,000 items of product A cost $10 and if in perfect condition can expected to be sold for $12 each. However 500 of these units are defective and can only be sold at $8 each

All units of product B cost $5 and are expected to sold for $3

The figure that should appear in Taylor's statement of financial position for inventory is $__________.

Enter a whole number WITHOUT the $ sign **(2 marks)**

13 Faith is a manufacturer of cars making two models, M1 and M2. At the year end 150 units of each model are in inventory.

Costs and related data for a unit of each model are as follows:

	M1	M2
	($)	($)
Costs to date	15,000	25,000
Selling Price	20,000	32,000
Modification costs to enable sale	4,500	
Marketing costs	700	750

The figure for inventory that should appear in the statement of financial position at the year end is $____________.

Enter a whole number WITHOUT the $ sign **(2 marks)**

14 A company values its inventory using the FIFO method. At 1 July 20X8 the company had 700 bottles of champagne in inventory valued at $56 each.

During the year ended 30 June 20X9 the following transactions took place:

1 September 20X8	Purchased 500 bottles of champagne at $60 each
20 October 20X8	Sold 650 bottles of champagne for $61,750
1 February 20X9	Purchased 200 bottles of champagne at $65 each
26 June 20X9	Sold 250 bottles of champagne for $26,250

The value of the company's closing inventory of champagne at 30 June 20X9 is $__________

Enter a whole number WITHOUT the $ sign **(2 marks)**

15 A business which is registered for sales tax received the following invoice from one of its sales tax registered suppliers:

Invoice number:	4829
Date:	29 February 20X4

Goods:	250 units @ $25	6,250.00
Less:	Trade discount	125.00
		6,125.00

The supplier has not charged sales tax on this purchase. He has also allowed a further discount of $250 if payment is received within 14 days. Sales tax is charged at 15%

The amount of sales tax that should have been charged on the invoice is $___________

Enter a whole number WITHOUT the $ sign **(2 marks)**

16 **The sales tax account in Olive's nominal ledger currently shows output tax and input tax for the quarter at $269,875 and $98,254 respectively.**

The amount payable to the tax authority is $__________.

Enter a whole number WITHOUT the $ sign **(1 mark)**

17 **Sarah is a sales tax registered trader whose sales and purchases carry sales tax at a rate of 15%. Sarah sells goods on credit for $5,500.00 inclusive of sales tax.**

The sales tax on this sale is $____________.

Enter a number to 2 decimal places WITHOUT the $ sign **(2 marks)**

18 **Taran sells goods to Kiren at a tax inclusive price of $890 and goods to Neeta at a tax exclusive price of $1,346.**

If the sales tax rate is 15%, the sales tax Taran is collecting on behalf of the government is $_________.

Enter a number to 2 decimal places WITHOUT the $ sign **(2 marks)**

19 **Vicky's business is registered for sales tax purposes. During the quarter ending 31 March 20X9 she made the following transactions that were all subject to sales tax at 15%.**

	Sales			Purchases	
1 January	$12,000	Excluding tax	5 January	$20,000	Excluding tax
1 February	$14,375	Including tax	31 January	$5,750	Including tax
1 March	$2,250	Excluding tax			

The balance on Vicky's sales tax account on 31 March 20X9 is $____________

Enter a number to 2 decimal places WITHOUT the $ sign **(2 marks)**

20 **A business has received telephone bills as follows:**

Quarter to:	Date Received	Bill ($)	Date Paid
30 November 20X7	December 20X7	672.81	January 20X8
28 February 20X8	March 20X8	875.26	April 20X8
31 May 20X8	June 20X8	894.35	June 20X8
31 August 20X8	September 20X8	799.32	September 20X8
30 November 20X8	December 20X8	840.47	January 20X9
28 February 20X9	March 20X9	955.86	March 20X9

In the statement of comprehensive income for the year ended 31 December 20X8 the charge for the telephone should be $___________.

Enter a number to 2 decimal places WITHOUT the $ sign **(2 marks)**

21 **Gloria has an insurance prepayment of $470 at 31 March 20X8. During the year ended 31 March 20X8 Gloria paid two insurance bills, one for $2,650 and one for $620.**

The income statement charge for insurance for the year ended 31 March 20X8 was $3,185. The prepayment at 31 March 20X7 was $___________.

Enter a whole number WITHOUT the $ sign **(2 marks)**

22 **The annual insurance premium for a sole trader for the period 1 July 20X7 to 30 June 20X8 is $24,510 which is 14% more than the previous year. Insurance premiums are paid on 1 July.**

The income statement charge for insurance for the year ended 31 December 20X7 is $_________.

Enter a whole number WITHOUT the $ sign **(2 marks)**

23 **Finch pays rent quarterly in advance on 1 January, 1 April, 1 July and 1 October each year. The annual rent increased from $120,000 per year to $144,000 per year as from 1 October 20X8.**

The rent expense charge that should appear in Finch's income statement for the year ended 31 July 20X9 is $______________

Enter a whole number WITHOUT the $ sign **(2 marks)**

24 **At 31 July 20X8, accrued rent payable was $500. During the year ended 31 July 20X9, rent paid was $7,200, including an invoice for $2,400 for the quarter ended 30 September 20X9.**

The income statement charge for rent payable for the year ended 31 July 20X9 is $________

Enter a whole number WITHOUT the $ sign **(2 marks)**

25 **Poppy's receivables totalled $800,000 at 31 December 20X7 and an allowance for receivables of $89,000 had been brought forward from the year ended 31 December 20X6.**

Debts totalling $76,000 are to written off and it was decided to adjust the allowance for receivables to $52,700.

The charge for irrecoverable debts that should appear in Poppy's income statement for the year ended 31 December 20X7 is $____________

Enter a whole number WITHOUT the $ sign **(2 marks)**

26 **At 31 March 20X5, Josh's allowance for receivables was $42,000. At 31 March 20X6 it was decided that $20,500 should be written off as an irrecoverable debt and to adjust the year end allowance to $38,000.**

The income statement charge for the year ended 31 March 20X6 for irrecoverable debts is $_____________.

Enter a whole number WITHOUT the $ sign **(2 marks)**

27 Barrett had an allowance for receivables at 1 September 20X3 of $25,000.

During the year ended 31 August 20X4 debts totalling $16,300 were written off. It was decided that the allowance for receivables should be increase to $27,500 as at 31 August 20X4.

The amount that should appear in Barrett's income statement for irrecoverable debt expense for the year ended 31 August 20X4 is $____________.

Enter a whole number WITHOUT the $ sign **(2 marks)**

28 At 30 April 20X5 Erin decided to write off two debts of $2,600 and $4,300 respectively and to adjust the year end allowance to $13,262. The balance on this allowance at 1 May 20X4 was $17,080.

Erin's irrecoverable debt expense for the year ended 30 April 20X5 is $__________.

Enter a whole number WITHOUT the $ sign **(2 marks)**

29 At 31 December 20X7 Suki's allowance for receivables was $39,000. At 31 December 20X8 trade receivables totalled $517,000. At this date it was decided to write off debts totalling $37,000 and to adjust the allowance for receivables to the equivalent of 5% of the trade receivables.

The figure that should appear in the income statement for irrecoverable debt expense for the year ended 31 December 20X8 is $_____________.

Enter a whole number WITHOUT the $ sign **(2 marks)**

30 The Rug Doctor purchased a van on 1 August 20X6 for a total cost of $28,000, paying $22,500 in cash and trading in an old van. The old van had cost $25,000 and the related accumulated depreciation was $15,600.

The loss on disposal in The Rug Doctor's income statement for the year ended 31 December 20X6 is $__________

Enter a whole number WITHOUT the $ sign **(2 marks)**

31 JBC purchases a machine for $30,000 on 1 January 20X8. After incurring transportation and installation costs of $2,600 and $5,000 respectively it breaks down and costs $1,200 to repair. Depreciation is charged on a straight line basis of 10% on cost.

The net book value of the machine shown in JBC's statement of financial position for the year ended 31 December 20X8 is $____________

Enter a whole number WITHOUT the $ sign **(2 marks)**

32 Charlie purchased a machine for $240,000 on 1 October 20X8. The estimated useful life of the asset is 8 years with a residual value of $8,000. Charlie uses the straight line method for depreciation and charges depreciation on a monthly basis.

The charge for depreciation for the year ended 31 December 20X8 is $_____________.

Enter a whole number WITHOUT the $ sign **(2 marks)**

33 **Sunil purchased an asset for $100,000 on 1 April 20X7. He charges depreciation of 25% on a reducing balance basis, charging a full years depreciation in the year of acquisition and none in the year of disposal.**

The net book value of the asset as at 31 December 20X9 is $__________.

Enter a number to 2 decimal places WITHOUT the $ sign **(2 marks)**

34 **Brian bought a machine for $10,000 on 1 January 20X3, when it had an expected useful life of four years and an expected residual value of $2,000. Depreciation was charged on a straight line basis, charging a full years depreciation in the year of acquisition and none in the year of disposal. On 20 April 20X6 Brian sold the machine for $2,600.**

The amount to be charged to the income statement for the loss on disposal for the year ended 31 December 20X6 is $____________

Enter a whole number WITHOUT the $ sign **(2 marks)**

35 **The correct double entry for a discount allowed is**

DR Discounts Allowed

CR ____________ Control Account.

Fill in blank with a single word, typed in lower case **(1 mark)**

36 **Sales tax on purchases from non credit suppliers is recorded in the book of prime entry known as the ____________ book**

Fill in blank with a single word, typed in lower case **(1 mark)**

37 **The receivables ledger at 1 August had balances of $65,500 debit and $2,550 credit. During August sales of $250,000 were made on credit. Receipts amounted to $245,000 and discounts of $1,100 were allowed. Refunds of $2,600 were made to customers.**

The net closing debit balance at 31 August on the receivables control account was $____________

Enter a whole number WITHOUT the $ sign **(2 marks)**

38 **Bruce maintains a receivables control account in the nominal ledger. At 30 September 20X8, the total of the list of individual balances extracted from the receivables ledger was $31,600, which did not agree with the balance on the receivables control account. An examination of the books revealed the following information, which can be used to reconcile the receivables ledger and the receivables control account.**

1 The personal account of Mahmood was undercast by $180

2 John's balance of $1,560 had been omitted from the list of balances

3 A credit note to Val for $2,000 plus VAT of $600, had been posted to the receivables control account as $2,600 but to Val's personal account as $2,000

4 The total on the credit side of Edward's personal account was overcast by $250.

The revised total of the balances in the receivables ledger after the errors have been corrected is $______________

Enter a whole number WITHOUT the $ sign **(2 marks)**

39 The following payables control account contains some errors. All goods are purchased on credit.

Payables Control Account

Purchases	968,500	Balance b/f	396,400
Discounts received	13,900	Cash paid to suppliers	1,101,700
Contra with receivables ledger	3,600		
Balance c/f	512,100		
	1,498,100		1,498,100

Once all the errors have been corrected the closing balance is $__________

Enter a whole number WITHOUT the $ sign **(2 marks)**

40 The following receivables control account contains some errors. All goods are sold on credit.

Receivables Control Account

Balance b/f	165,000	Credit sales	228,000
Cash from credit customers	365,000	Irrecoverable debts written off	900
Cash refunds to credit customers	2,700	Contras against payables ledger	5,200
Discounts allowed	5,300	Balance c/f	303,900
	538,000		538,000

Once all the errors have been corrected the closing balance is $__________

Enter a whole number WITHOUT the $ sign **(2 marks)**

41 The following payables control account contains some errors. All goods are purchased on credit.

Payables Control Account

Balance b/f (amount owing to suppliers)	427,000	Purchases	1,566,000
Cash paid to suppliers	1,870,400	Contras against receivables ledger	46,000
Refunds received from suppliers	4,000	Discounts received	9,700
		Balance c/f	679,700
	2,301,400		2,301,400

Once all the errors have been corrected the closing balance is $__________

Enter a whole number WITHOUT the $ sign **(2 marks)**

42 **A receivables control account had a closing balance of $9,200. It contained a contra to the payables ledger of $600, but this had been entered on the wrong side of the control account.**

The correct closing debit balance on the control account is $________________

Enter a whole number WITHOUT the $ sign **(2 marks)**

43 **The balance on Sam's cash book is $54 overdrawn. His bank statement shows that he is $1,250 in credit. When Sam does a reconciliation he finds that there are unpresented cheques of $654, unrecorded direct debits of $400 and a customer has paid $1,050 directly into his bank account.**

His cash book balance should be $________________

Enter a whole number WITHOUT the $ sign **(2 marks)**

44 **Connie's cash book at 31 May 20X7 shows a balance at the bank of $4,980. A comparison with her bank statement at the same date reveals the following differences:**

Unpresented cheques	1,680
Bank charges not recorded in the cash book	100
Receipts not yet credited by the bank	940
Dishonoured cheques	280

The correct cash book balance at 31 May 20X7 is $________________

Enter a whole number WITHOUT the $ sign **(2 marks)**

45 **A bank statement on 31 December 20X8 showed an overdraft of $1,600. On reconciling the bank statement, it was discovered that a cheque drawn for $160 had not been presented for payment, and a cheque for $260 from a customer had been dishonoured, but the company had not yet been notified.**

The correct bank overdraft to be shown in the statement of financial position at 31 December 20X8 is $________________

Enter a whole number WITHOUT the $ sign **(2 marks)**

46 **The cash book shows a bank balance of $6,535 overdrawn at 30 September 20X7. It is subsequently discovered that a standing order payment for $250 has been entered twice, and that a dishonoured cheque for $550 has been debited in the cash book instead of credited.**

The correct bank overdraft as at 30 September 20X7 should be $________________

Enter a whole number WITHOUT the $ and – sign (2 marks)

47 Suki's cash book at 30 April 20X6 shows a bank balance of $656 overdrawn. On comparing this with his bank statement at the same date he discovers the following:

1 A cheque for $86 from a customer which was paid into the bank on 23 April has been dishonoured

2 A cheque for $32 drawn by Suki on 29 April has not yet been presented for payment.

The correct overdraft to be shown in the statement of financial position as at 30 April 20X6 is $_____________

Enter a whole number WITHOUT the $ and – sign (2 marks)

48 A suspense account was opened when a trial balance failed to agree. The following errors were later discovered.

1 A telephone bill of $320 had been recorded in the telephone expense account as $230

2 A discount of $100 received had been debited to discounts allowed

3 Interest paid of $40 had been entered in the bank account only

The original credit balance on the suspense account was $_____________

Enter a whole number WITHOUT the $ sign **(2 marks)**

49 An error of _________________ is one where one side of the transaction has been recorded in the wrong account, and that account is of the same class as the correct account.

Fill in blank with a single word, typed in lower case **(1 marks)**

50 An error is identified where a discount received of $1,684 has been debited to both the payables control account and the discounts received account. The double entry required to correct this is

DR Suspense

CR Discounts Received

The amount that should be recorded in the journal to correct the error is $___________

Enter a whole number WITHOUT the $ sign **(2 marks)**

51 Alex only buys inventories on credit. At 31 May 20X8 the payables control account and the list of payables ledger balances fail to agree.

A contra of $876 has only been recorded in Alex's ledger account for its supplier Jack.

In the payables control account reconciliation the control account balance should be reduced by $_______________ ?

Enter a whole number WITHOUT the $ sign **(1 marks)**

52 **Michael only buys inventories on credit. At 31 January 20X9 the payables control account and the list of payables ledger balances fail to agree.**

An invoice of $912 from Finch has been recorded as a credit note in the purchase day book. In the payables control account reconciliation both the control account balance and the list of balances should be increased by $_______________.

Enter a whole number WITHOUT the $ sign **(2 marks)**

53 **Wilson has lost some of his accounting records but has the following information:**

Payables at 1 March 20X9	15,000
Payables at 31 March 20X9	9,000
Total payments during March	
(including cash payments of $250)	12,300

Purchases made on credit during March 20X9 amount to $_______________

Enter a whole number WITHOUT the $ sign **(2 marks)**

54 **If sales are $192,000 and gross profit margin is 25% the value of cost of sales is $___________**

Enter a whole number WITHOUT the $ sign **(1 mark)**

55 **During February, Frank had sales of $222,000, which made a gross profit of $60,000. On 1 February the value of opening inventory was $51,000 and during the month purchases amounted to $150,000**

The value of closing inventory at 28 February was $_______________

Enter a whole number WITHOUT the $ sign **(2 marks)**

56 **Mark's receivables control account has a balance at 1 June 20X7 of $180,000 debit. During the month of June cash received from credit customers was $228,000, cash refunds to credit customers were $3,300 and discounts allowed were $4,200. However it was discovered that a customer, Matt had left the country and therefore his debt of $1,500 was written off as irrecoverable. Contras against payables amounted to $2,400 for the month.**

The closing balance on the receivables control account at 30 June 20X7 was $129,200.

The total credit sales for the month of June was $_______________

Enter a whole number WITHOUT the $ sign **(2 marks)**

57 **Alice and Becky are in partnership, sharing profits and losses in the ratio 2:1. Their year end is 30 June.**

On 1 January 20X7 Clare joined the partnership and the new profit sharing ratio became 5:3:2.

The profit for the year ended 30 June 20X7 was $675,000, after charging an expense of $60,000 related to the first 6 months of the year. The remainder of the profit accrued evenly over the year.

Becky's total profit share for the year ended 30 June 20X7 is $______________

Enter a whole number WITHOUT the $ sign **(2 marks)**

58 **Derek, Jin and Ahmed are in business together sharing profits in the ratio 3:3:4 after providing for salaries for Derek and Jin of $20,000 and $24,000 respectively. The partners each receive interest of 8% per annum on their capital balances and pay interest of 10% on their drawings. The profit for the year to 31 March 20X8 is $254,000 before providing for salaries or interest.**

The partners' capital balances and drawings are as follows:

	Capital balance	Drawings on 1 April 20X7
	$	$
Derek	100,000	46,000
Jin	90,000	38,000
Ahmed	132,000	48,000
Total	322,000	132,000

Jin's total profit share for the year ended 31 March 20X8 is $______________

Enter a whole number WITHOUT the $ sign **(2 marks)**

59 **Fred and Jim are in partnership sharing profits equally and compiling financial statements to 31 December each year.**

They both are paid a salary of $20,000 each year. They receive 5% interest on their capital balances and pay interest of 10% per annum on their drawings.

Fred has $56,000 invested in the partnership and Jim has $125,000. Fred took $25,000 out of the business on the 1 April 20X8 and a further $12,000 on 1 September 20X8.The profit for the year ended 31 December 20X8 is $182,225 before providing for salaries and interest.

Fred's total profit share for the year ended 31 December 20X8 is $____________

Enter a whole number WITHOUT the $ sign **(2 marks)**

60 **Faith, Hope and Charity are partners sharing profits in the ratio 1:2:3. The partnership agreement provides for interest on capital at the rate of 6% per annum and a salary for Faith of $9,000 per annum. Profit for the year for 20X6 was $84,000 and the balances on partners' capital accounts throughout the year were: Faith $20,000; Hope $15,000; Charity $12,000.**

Faith's share of profits for 20X6 is $____________

Enter a whole number WITHOUT the $ sign **(2 marks)**

61 **Peter and Quentin are in partnership, sharing profit in the ratio 2:1. On 1 July 20X8 Robert joined the partnership. Peter guaranteed that Robert's profit share would not be less than $50,000 for the 6 months to 31 December 20X8. The new partnership agreement states that profit should be shared in the ratio 5:3:2. The profit for the year ended 31 December 20X8 is $480,000, accruing evenly over the year.**

Peter's final profit share for the year ended 31 December 20X8 is $____________

Enter a whole number WITHOUT the $ sign **(2 marks)**

62 **The issued share capital of Golden plc is as follows:**

	$
Ordinary shares of 20 cents each	1,000,000
8% preference shares of 50 cents each	500,000

In the year ended 30 September 20X7, the company paid the preference dividend for the year and an interim dividend of 3 cents per share on the ordinary shares. A final ordinary dividend of 5 cents per share was declared on 29 September 20X7

The total amount of dividends accounted for in the year ended 30 September 20X7 is $__________

Enter a whole number WITHOUT the $ sign **(2 marks)**

63 **At 31 December 20X8 the capital structure of a company was as follows:**

	$
200,000 ordinary shares of $0.50 each	100,000
Share premium account	360,000

During 20X9, the company made a 1 for 2 bonus issue, using the share premium account for the purpose, and later issued for cash another 120,000 shares at $1.60 per share.

The balance on the company's share premium account as at 31 December 20X9 is $____________

Enter a whole number WITHOUT the $ sign **(2 marks)**

64 A company has the following capital structure:

	$
400,000 shares of $0.25	100,000
Share premium account	150,000

It makes a 1 for 5 rights issue at $1.45, which is fully subscribed.

The balance on the share premium account following the rights issue is $____________

Enter a whole number WITHOUT the $ sign **(2 marks)**

65 During the year to 31 March 20X8, Maggie plc had issued share capital of 500,000 ordinary shares of $0.50 each and 100,000 $1 9% preference shares.

An interim ordinary dividend of $0.05 per share and the full preference dividend were paid during the year. On 2 April 20X8 a final ordinary dividend of $0.15 per share was declared.

The total dividends accounted for in the year ended 31 March 20X8 are $__________

Enter a whole number WITHOUT the $ sign **(2 marks)**

66 A company is preparing its financial statements for the year ending 31 March 20X8. The initial trial balance has the following figures relating to tax:

Tax payable at 1 April 20X7	28,600
Tax paid during the year ended 31 March 20X8	25,400

The estimated tax liability for the year ended 31 March 20X8 is $31,200

The figure for the tax expense in the company's income statement will be $__________

Enter a whole number WITHOUT the $ sign **(2 marks)**

67 Extracts from the accounts of Rose showed balances as follows:

	20X7	20X6
$0.50 share capital	450,000	180,000
Share premium	390,000	150,000

A bonus issue of 1 share for every 15 held at the 20X6 year end occurred during the year and loan notes of $525,000 were issued at par. Interest of $18,000 was paid during the year.

The next cash inflow from financing activities is $____________

Enter a whole number WITHOUT the $ sign **(2 marks)**

68 **Violet plc made a profit before tax of $239,000. The income statement at the year end shows a finance charge of $36,000 and investment income of $55,000. Assets were depreciated by $98,000 and no acquisitions or disposals were made.**

Extracts from Violet's statement of financial position are as follows:

	20X8	**20X7**
Current Assets		
Inventory	76,000	52,000
Receivables	89,000	95,500
Dividend receivable	12,300	14,900
Cash	1,200	5,725
Current Liabilities		
Trade payables	51,250	43,800
Dividend payable	19,000	21,200
Tax	45,000	54,000

The cash generated from operations (using the indirect method) is $_____________

Enter a whole number WITHOUT the $ sign **(2 marks)**

69 **On 1 January 20X8 Lily had property, plant and equipment with a book value of $250,000 and motor vehicles with a book value of $30,000. During the year a vehicle was sold that had cost $12,000 and had been depreciated by $2,400. Depreciation for the year was $42,500. The total book value of assets at the year end was $296,000.**

The total amount of cash that had been invested in non-current assets during the year was $_____________

Enter a whole number WITHOUT the $ sign **(2 marks)**

70 **The statements of financial position for Hyacinth, a limited liability company, as at 31 October 20X8 and 20X9 showed declared dividends of $780,000 and $520,000 respectively.**

The retained earnings for the year ended 31 October 20X9 showed dividends of $960,000.

The amount that should be shown in the statement of cash flows for the year ended 31 October 20X9 is $_____________

Enter a whole number WITHOUT the $ sign **(2 marks)**

Section 4

ANSWERS TO OBJECTIVE TEST QUESTIONS

1 ASSET

2 DRAWINGS

The accounting equation, assets = liabilities + opening capital + profit – drawings can be rewritten as:

Assets – liabilities – opening capital +drawings = profit

3 LIABILITIES

Liabilities are items that we owe. Payables is money owed to our suppliers, tax is owed to the relevant tax authority, loans and overdrafts are money owed to the bank or other lenders.

4 LIABILITIES

Assets increase as cash on receipt on receipt of the loan funds and liabilities will increase as the loan will need to be repaid in the future and hence is a liability.

5 CAPITAL

The car increases non-current assets as it is intended for continued use in the business and is treated as capital introduced as it is will increase the amount owed by the business to the owner.

6 13,700

Receivables

Balance b/f	5,400	Receipts	24,700
Sales	33,000	Balance c/f	13,700
	38,400		38,400

7 125

Cash

Cash sales	125	Purchases	960
		Drawings	62

DR	Purchases	960
CR	Cash	960
DR	Receivables	500
CR	Sales	500

As the customer pays in the following month it will not impact on the current months cash T-account.

DR	Drawings	62
CR	Cash	62

8 216,429

Payables

		Balance b/f	28,682
Payments	216,429	Purchases	222,602
Balance c/f	34,855		
	251,284		251,284

Remember: the payables ledger does not include cash purchases so it is important that the cash purchases are deducted from total purchases.

9 ALLOWED

Discounts allowed are given to credit customers to encourage prompt payment. They are treated as an expense of the period.

10 11,220

Capital

		Balance b/f	8,200
Drawings	1,800	Profit	4,820
Balance c/f	11,220		
	13,020		13,020

11 1,184

Date	Units	Cost / unit ($)	Total Cost ($)
1 March	60	12	720
12 March	40	15	600
18 March	50	18	900
	150		2,220

Average cost per unit	=	$2,220 / 150
	=	$14.80
Inventory remaining at 31 March 20X9	=	150 -70
	=	80
Value of closing inventory	=	80 x $14.80
	=	$1,184

12 65,000

Product A

5,500 units @ $10	=	55,000
500 units @ $8	=	4,000
Total		59,000

Product B

2,000 units @ $3 = 6,000

Total value of closing inventory = $59,000 + $6,000

= $65,000

Inventory should be valued at the lower of cost and net realisable value (NRV). In the case of product A the 500 defective units should be valued at NRV however the 5,500 units that are in perfect condition should be valued at cost.

All units of product B should be valued at $3

13 5,970,000

	M1		**M2**
Cost	$15,000	Cost	$25,000
NRV	$14,800 (20,000 – 4,500 -700)	NRV	$31,250 (32,000 – 750)

150 units valued at NRV = 150 × $14,800
= $2,220,000

150 units valued at cost = 150 × $25,000
= $3,750,000

Total inventory value = $2,220,000 + $3,750,000
= $5,970,000

Note: NRV is the revenue expected to be earned in the future when goods are sold less any selling costs. In this case both the modification costs and marketing costs would be classed as selling costs so should be deducted from the selling price to calculate NRV.

14 31,000

1 July 20X8	700 @ $56	39,200
1 September 20X8	500 @ $60	30,000
20 October 20X8	(650 @ $56)	(36,400)
1 February 20X9	200 @ $65	13,000
26 June 20X9	(50 @ $56)	(2,800)
	(200 @ $60)	(12,000)
		31,000

15 881.25

Goods:	250 units @ $25	6,250.00
Less:	Trade discount	125.00
Less:	Settlement Discount	250.00
		5,875.00
Sales Tax at 15%		881.25

Note: When calculating sales tax on invoices we always assume that any settlement discounts will be taken.

16 171,621

Sales Tax

Input tax	98,254		
		Output tax	269,875
Balance c/f	171,621		
	269,875		269,875

Note: Output tax is tax on sales and therefore owed to the tax authority. Input tax is tax on purchases and can be reclaimed from the tax authority i.e. reduces the tax liability and therefore the amount owed.

17 717.39

$5,500.00 x (15 / 115) = $717.39

18 317.99

Sales to Kiren (tax inclusive)	$890 x (15 / 115)	=	$116.09
Sales to Neeta (tax exclusive)	$1,346 x (15 / 100)	=	$201.90
		TOTAL	$317.99

19 262.50

Sales Tax

5 Jan	3000.00	1 Jan	1,800.00
31 Jan	750.00	1 Feb	1,875.00
Balance c/f	262.50	1 March	337.50
	4,012.50		4,012.50

Workings:

	Sales		Purchases
1 January	$12,000 excluding tax	5 January	$20,000 excluding tax
	$12,000 x (15 / 100)		$20,000 x (15 / 100)
	= $1,800.00		= $3,000.00
1 February	$14,375 including tax	31 January	$5,750 including tax
	$14,375 x (15 / 115)		$5,750 x (15 / 115)
	= $1,875.00		= $750.00
1 March	$2,250 excluding tax		
	$2,250 x (15 / 100)		
	= $337.50		

20 3436.27

Quarter to:	Bill ($)	Months relevant to yr ended 31/12/X8	Charge ($)	
30 November 20X7	672.81	0		
28 February 20X8	875.26	2	583.51	(875.26 x 2/3)
31 May 20X8	894.35	3	894.35	
31 August 20X8	799.32	3	799.32	
30 November 20X8	840.47	3	840.47	
28 February 20X9	955.86	1	318.62	(955.86 x 1/3)
		TOTAL	3,436.27	

Note: We account for transactions in the period to which they relate not when the cash is received or paid.

21 385

Insurance Expense

Opening prepayment (β)	385	Income Statement	3,185
Bill	2,650		
Bill	620	Closing prepayment	470
	3,655		3,655

22 23,005

1 January 20X7 – 30 June 20X7	($24,510 / 1.14) x 6/12	= $10,750
1 July 20X7 – 31 December 20X7	$24,510 x 6/12	= $12,255
	TOTAL	$23,005

23 140,000

1 August 20X8 – 31 September 20X8	$120,000 x 2/12	= $ 20,000
1 October 20X8 – 31 July 20X9	$144,000 x 10/12	= $120,000
	TOTAL	$140,000

24 5,100 (5,100)

Rent Expense

		Opening accrual	500
Payment	7,200	Income Statement	5,100
		Closing prepayment	1,600
	7,200		7,200

Prepayment Working:

$2,400 x 2/3 = $1,600

25 39,700

Allowance for receivables

		Balance b/f	89,000
Irrecoverable Debt Expense	36,300		
Balance c/f	52,700		
	89,000		89,000

Irrecoverable debt Expense

Irrecoverable Debt Written Off	76,000	Allowance for Receivables	36,300
		Income Statement	39,700
	76,000		76,000

26 16,500

Allowance for Receivables

		Balance b/f	42,000
Irrecoverable Debt Expense	4,000		
Balance c/f	38,000		
	42,000		42,000

Irrecoverable Debt Expense

Irrecoverable Debt Written Off	20,500	Allowance for Receivables	4,000
		Income Statement	16,500
	20,500		20,500

27 18,800

Allowance for Receivables

		Balance b/f	25,000
		Irrecoverable Debt Expense	2,500
Balance c/f	27,500		
	27,500		27,500

Irrecoverable Debt Expense

Irrecoverable Debt Written Off	16,300		
Allowance for Receivables	2,500	Income Statement	18,800
	18,800		18,800

28 3,082

Allowance for Receivables

		Balance b/f	17,080
Irrecoverable Debt Expense	3,818		
Balance c/f	13,262		
	17,080		17,080

Irrecoverable Debt Expense

Irrecoverable Debt Written Off	6,900	Allowance for Receivables	3,818
		Income Statement	3,082
	6,900		6,900

29 22,000

Allowance for Receivables

		Balance b/f	39,000
Irrecoverable Debt Expense	15,000		
Balance c/f	24,000		
	39,000		39,000

Irrecoverable Debt Expense

Irrecoverable Debt Written Off	37,000	Allowance for Receivables	15,000
		Income Statement	22,000
	37,000		37,000

Allowance working:

Receivables @ 31 December 20X8	517,000
Irrecoverable debt written off	37,000
	480,000
General Allowance (5%)	24,000

30 3,900

Disposal

Cost	25,000	Accumulated Depreciation	15,600
		Part Exchange Allowance	5,500
		Loss on disposal	3,900
	25,000		25,000

31

Cost	$
Purchase	30,000
Transportation	2,600
Installation	5,000
	37,600
Less Depreciation (10%)	3,760
Net Book Value	33,840

Repair costs are classed as revenue expenditure and therefore are not included as part of the cost of the non-current asset.

The purchase cost, transportation cost and installation cost are all capital expenditure and are treated as part of the cost of the non-current asset.

32 9,750

Annual depreciation charge	=	(cost – residual value) / useful life
(240,000 – 8,000) / 8 years	=	$29,000
Depreciation charge for 20X8	=	$29,000 x 3/12
	=	$7,250

33 42,187.50

Year	Depreciation	Net Book Value
20X7	100,000 x 25% = 25,000.00	75,000.00
20X8	75,000 x 25% = 18,750.00	56,250.00
20X9	56,250 x 25% = 14,062.50	42,187.50

34 1,400

Annual depreciation	=	(10,000-2,000) / 4
	=	$2,000
NBV at disposal	=	10,000 – (2,000 x 3)
	=	4,000
Loss on disposal	=	NBV – Proceeds
	=	4,000 – 2,600
	=	1,400

35 RECEIVABLES

Discounts allowed are given on credit sales and therefore are recorded in the receivables control account

36 CASH

When transactions take place in cash they must be recorded in the cash book.

37 69,450

Receivables Control Account

Balance b/f	65,500	Balance b/f	2,550
Sales	250,000	Receipts	245,000
Refunds	2,600	Discounts Allowed	1,100
		Balance c/f	69,450
	318,100		318,100

38 32,900

List of balances	31,600
Mahmood	180
John	1,560
Val	(600)
Edward	250
Revised total	32,990

39 245,700

Payables Control Account

Cash paid to suppliers	1,101,700	Balance b/f	396,400
Discounts received	13,900		
Contra with receivables ledger	3,600	Purchases	968,500
Balance c/f	245,700		
	1,364,900		1,364,900

40 19,300

Receivables Control Account

Balance b/f	165,000	Cash from credit customers	365,000
Credit sales	228,000	Irrecoverable debts written off	900
Cash refunds to credit customers	2,700	Contras against payables ledger	5,200
		Discounts allowed	5,300
		Balance c/f	19,300
	395,700		395,700

41 70,900

Payables Control Account

Cash paid to suppliers	1,870,400	Balance b/f (amount owing to suppliers)	427,000
Contras against receivables ledger	46,000	Purchases	1,566,000
Discounts received	9,700	Refunds received from suppliers	4,000
Balance c/f	70,900		
	1,997,000		1,997,000

42 8,000

\$9,200 – (\$600 x 2) = \$8,000

43 596

	\$
Cash book balance	(54)
Unrecorded direct debit	(400)
Unrecorded receipt	1,050
Revised cash book balance	596

Note: the unpresented cheques would already have been recorded in the cash book.

44 4,600

Bank balance	4,980
Bank charges not recorded	(100)
Dishonoured cheques	(280)
Revised cash book balance	4,600

Note: unpresented cheques and receipts not credited by the bank would already have been recorded in the cash book.

45 1,760

Overdraft	(1,600)
Cheque drawn	(160)
	(1,760)

The dishonoured cheque will only have an effect on the cash book not on the bank statement.

46 7,385

	\$
Cash book balance	(6,535)
Correction of standing order	250
Correction of dishonoured cheque	(1,100)
	(7,385)

47 742

Cash book balance	(656)
Dishonoured cheque	(86)
Revised cash book balance	(742)

48 70

	Did do			Should do	
1	DR telephone expense	230	DR	telephone expense	320
	DR suspense	90	CR	bank	320
	CR bank	320			
2	DR payables	100	DR	payables	100
	DR discounts allowed	100	CR	discounts received	100
	CR suspense	200			
3	DR suspense	40	DR	interest paid	40
	CR bank	40	CR	bank	40

Suspense

Telephone	90	Discount	200
Interest	40		
Opening balance	**70**		
	200		200

49 COMMISSION

An error of commission is where a transaction has been recorded in the wrong account, for example rent expense of $500 is recorded as telephone expense

50 3,368

Did do			Should do		
DR	Payables control account	1,684	DR	Payables control account	1,684
DR	Discounts received	1,684	CR	Discounts received	1,684
CR	Suspense	3,368			
Correction					
DR	Suspense	3,368			
CR	Discounts received	3,368			

51 876

The contra was debited to the payables ledger account so it should also have been debited to the control account, to reduce it by $876

52 1,824

$912 should have credited to payables but instead it was debited. Therefore both the control account and the memorandum ledger will be incorrect and should be credited with $912 to correct the error and $912 again to record the invoice ($912 x 2)

53 6,050

Payables

		Balance b/f	15,000
Payments	12,050		
		Credit purchases	6,050
Balance c/f	9,000		
	21,050		21,050

54 144,000

	$	
Sales	192,000	100%
Cost of Sales	144,000	75%
Gross Profit	48,000	25%

55 39,000

	$	$
Sales		222,000
Cost of sales		
Opening inventory	51,000	
Purchases	150,000	
Closing Inventory	39,000	
		162,000
Gross Profit		60,000

56 182,000

Receivables control account

Balance b/f	180,000	Cash received	228,000
Cash refunds	3,300	Discounts allowed	4,200
Credit sales	182,000	Irrecoverable debt written off	1,500
		Contra with payables	2,400
		Balance c/f	129,200
	365,300		365,300

57 222,750

Profit for year = $675,000 + $60,000

= $735,000

	Alice	Becky	Clare
1 July 20X6 – 31 December 20X6			
(735,000 – 60,000) x 6/12	225,000	112,500	
shared in ratio 2:1			
1 January 20X7 – 30 June 20X7			
735,000 x 6/12 shared in ratio 5:3:2	183,750	110,250	73,500
	———	———	———
Total	408,750	222,750	73,500

58 86,632

	Derek	Jin	Ahmed	Total
	$	$	$	$
Salaries	20,000	24,000		44,000
Interest on capital	8,000	7,200	10,560	25,760
Interest on drawings	(4,600)	(3,800)	(4,800)	(13,200)
Profit share (3:3:4)	59,232	59,232	78,976	197,440
	———	———	———	———
	82,632	86,632	84,736	254,000

59 88,250

	Fred	Jim	Total
	$	$	$
Salaries	20,000	20,000	40,000
Interest on capital	2,800	6,250	9,050
Interest on drawings	(2,275)		(2,275)
Profit share (1:1)	67,725	67,725	135,450
	———	———	———
	88,250	93,975	182,225

Interest on drawings

1 April 20X8 25,000 x 10% x 9/12 = $1,875

1 September 20X8 12,000 x 10% x 4/12 = $400

60 22,230

	Faith	Hope	Charity	Total
	$	$	$	$
Salaries	9,000			9,000
Interest on capital	1,200	900	720	2,820
Profit share (1:2:3)	12,030	24,060	36,090	72,180
	22,230	24,960	36,810	84,000

61 278,750

	Peter	Quentin	Robert	Total
	$	$	$	$
1 January – 30 June (480,000 x 6/12) 2:1	160,000	80,000	240,000	
1 July – 31 December (480,000 x 6/12) 5:3:2	120,000	72,000	48,000	240,000
Total	280,000	152,000	48,000	480,000
GMPS 2,000 5:3	(1,250)	(750)	2,000	
	278,750	151,250	50,000	480,000

62 440,000

$1,000,000 20 cent shares = 5,000,000 shares

Interim dividend of 3 cents per share	5,0000,000 x $0.03 = 150,000
Final dividend of 5 cents per share	5,000,000 x $0.05 = 250,000
Preference share dividend	500,000 x 8% = 40,000

Total: 150,000 + 250,000 + 40,000 = 440,000

63

Share Premium

Bonus issue	50,000	Balance b/f	360,000
		Issue	132,000
Balance c/f	442,000		
	492,000		492,000

1 for 2 bonus issue = 200,000 shares ×1/2 @ $0.50 each

= $50,000

New issue: 120,000 shares @ $1.60

Share capital account = 120,000 x $0.50

Share premium account = 120,000 x ($1.60 - $0.50)

64 246,000

Share Premium

		Balance b/f	150,000
		Rights Issue	96,000
Balance c/f	246,000		
	246,000		246,000

1 for 5 rights issue = 80,000 shares @ $1.45

Share capital account = 80,000 x $0.25

Share premium account = 80,000 x ($1.45 - $0.25)

65 34,000

Interim dividend of 5 cents per share	500,000 x $0.05	=	25,000
Preference share dividend	100,000 x 9%	=	9,000

Total: 25,000 + 9,000 = 34,000

Note: ordinary dividends declared after the year end are accounted for in the following accounting period. In this case the final dividend of $0.15 per share will be accounted for in the year ended 31 March 20X9.

66 28,000

Tax Payable

Tax paid	25,400	Balance b/f	28,600
		Income statement	28,000
Balance c/f	31,200		
	56,600		56,600

67 1,035,000

	$
Issue of shares (450,000 – 180,000 + 390,000 – 150,000)	510,000
Issue of loan notes	525,000
Total	1,035,000

The interest paid is excluded from the answer as it is accounted for under 'operating activities'

68 307,950

	$
Profit before tax	239,000
Finance cost	36,000
Investment income	(55,000)
Depreciation charge	98,000
Increase in inventory	(24,000)
Decrease in receivables	6,500
Increase in payables	7,450
Cash generated from operations	307,950

69

Non-current assets at NBV

Balance b/f	280,000	Disposal (12,000 – 2,400)	9,600
(250 + 30)		Depreciation	42,500
Additions	68,100	Balance c/f	296,000
	348,100		348,100

70 1,220,000

	$
Opening declared dividends	780,000
Dividends for the year	960,000
Closing declared dividends	(520,000)
Total dividends paid	1,220,000

Section 5

PILOT PAPER EXAM QUESTIONS

1 **Should details of material adjusting or material non-adjusting events after the reporting date be disclosed in the notes to financial statements according to IAS 10 *Events After the Reporting Date*?**

A Adjusting events

B Non-adjusting events **(1 mark)**

2 **At 30 June 2005 a company's allowance for receivables was $39,000. At 30 June 2006 trade receivables totalled $517,000. It was decided to write off debts totalling $37,000 and to adjust the allowance for receivables to the equivalent of 5 per cent of the trade receivables based on past events.**

What figure should appear in the income statement for the year ended 30 June 2006 for these items?

A $61,000

B $22,000

C $24,000

D $23,850 **(2 marks)**

3 **In times of rising prices, what effect does the use of the historical cost concept have on a company's asset values and profit?**

A Asset values and profit both understated

B Asset values and profit both overstated

C Asset values understated and profit overstated

D Asset values overstated and profit understated **(2 marks)**

4 **The IASB's Framework for the preparation and presentation of financial statements gives qualitative characteristics that make financial information reliable.**

Which of the following are examples of those qualitative characteristics?

A Faithful representation, neutrality and prudence

B Neutrality, comparability and true and fair view

C Prudence, comparability and accruals

D Neutrality, accruals and going concern **(2 marks)**

5 The following bank reconciliation statement has been prepared by a trainee accountant:

	$
Overdraft per bank statement	3,860
Less: Outstanding cheques	9,160
	5,300
Add: Deposits credited after date	16,690
Cash at bank as calculated above	21,990

What should be the correct balance per the cash book?

A $21,990 balance at bank as stated

B $3,670 balance at bank

C $11,390 balance at bank

D $3,670 overdrawn **(2 marks)**

6 Which of the following calculates a trader's net profit for a period?

A Closing net assets + drawings – capital introduced – opening net assets

B Closing net assets – drawings + capital introduced – opening net assets

C Closing net assets – drawings – capital introduced – opening net assets

D Closing net assets + drawings + capital introduced – opening net assets **(2 marks)**

7 A sole trader took some goods costing $800 from inventory for his own use. The normal selling price of the goods is $1,600.

Which of the following journal entries would correctly record this?

		Dr $	*Cr* $
A	Drawings account	800	
	Inventory account		800
B	Drawings account	800	
	Purchases account		800
C	Sales account	1,600	
	Drawings account		1,600

(1 mark)

8 The debit side of a company's trial balance totals $800 more than the credit side.

Which one of the following errors would fully account for the difference?

A $400 paid for plant maintenance has been correctly entered in the cash book and credited to the plant asset account

B Discount received $400 has been debited to discount allowed account

C A receipt of $800 for commission receivable has been omitted from the records

D The petty cash balance of $800 has been omitted from the trial balance **(2 marks)**

9 A company's statement of comprehensive income for the year ended 31 December 2005 showed a net profit of $83,600. It was later found that $18,000 paid for the purchase of a motor van had been debited to the motor expenses account. It is the company's policy to depreciate motor vans at 25 per cent per year on the straight line basis, with a full year's charge in the year of acquisition.

What would the net profit be after adjusting for this error?

A $106,100

B $70,100

C $97,100

D $101,600 **(2 marks)**

10 Should dividends paid appear on the face of a company's statement of comprehensive income?

A Yes

B No **(1 mark)**

11 The following control account has been prepared by a trainee accountant:

Receivables ledger control account

	$		$
Opening balance	308,600	Cash received from credit customers	147,200
Credit sales	154,200	Discounts allowed to credit customers	1,400
Cash sales	88,100	Interest charged on overdue accounts	2,400
Contras against credit balances in payables ledger	4,600	Bad debts written off	4,900
		Allowance for receivables	2,800
		Closing balance	396,800
	555,500		555,500

What should the closing balance be when all the errors made in preparing the receivables ledger control account have been corrected?

A $395,200

B $304,300

C $309,500

D $307,100 **(2 marks)**

12 **At 31 December 2004 Q, a limited liability company, owned a building that cost $800,000 on 1 January 1995. It was being depreciated at two per cent per year.**

On 1 January 2005 ,a revaluation to $1,000,000 was recognised. At this date the building had a remaining useful life of 40 years.

What is the depreciation charge for the year ended 31 December 2005 and the revaluation reserve balance as at 1 January 2005?

	Depreciation charge for year ended 31 December 2005	*Revaluation reserve as at 1 January 2005*
	$	$
A	25,000	200,000
B	25,000	360,000
C	20,000	200,000
D	20,000	360,000

(2 marks)

13 **P and Q are in partnership, sharing profits equally.**

On 30 June 2005, R joined the partnership and it was agreed that from that date all three partners should share equally in the profit.

In the year ended 31 December 2005 the profit amounted to $300,000, accruing evenly over the year, after charging a bad debt of $30,000 which it was agreed should be borne equally by P and Q only.

What should P's total profit share be for the year ended 31 December 2005?

A $95,000

B $122,500

C $125,000

D $110,000 **(2 marks)**

14 **A company has made a material change to an accounting policy in preparing its current financial statements.**

Which of the following disclosures are required by IAS 8 Accounting policies, changes in accounting estimates and errors in the financial statements?

1 The reasons for the change.

2 The amount of the adjustment in the current period and in comparative information for prior periods.

3 An estimate of the effect of the change on the next five accounting periods.

A 1 and 2 only

B 1 and 3 only

C 2 and 3 only

D 1, 2 and 3 **(2 marks)**

15 According to IAS 2 *Inventories*, which of the following costs should be included in valuing the inventories of a manufacturing company?

(1) Carriage inwards.

(2) Carriage outwards.

(3) Depreciation of factory plant.

(4) General administrative overheads.

A All four items

B 1, 2 and 4 only

C 2 and 3 only

D 1 and 3 only **(2 marks)**

16 Part of a company's statement of cash flows is shown below:

	$000
Operating profit	8,640
Depreciation charges	(2,160)
Increase in inventory	(330)
Increase in accounts payable	440

The following criticisms of the extract have been made:

(1) Depreciation charges should have been added, not deducted.

(2) Increase in inventory should have been added, not deducted.

(3) Increase in accounts payable should have been deducted, not added.

Which of the criticisms are valid?

A 2 and 3 only

B 1 only

C 1 and 3 only

D 2 only **(2 marks)**

17 Which of the following explains the imprest system of operating petty cash?

A Weekly expenditure cannot exceed a set amount

B The exact amount of expenditure is reimbursed at intervals to maintain a fixed float

C All expenditure out of the petty cash must be properly authorised

D Regular equal amounts of cash are transferred into petty cash at intervals **(2 marks)**

18 Which of the following are differences between sole traders and limited liability companies?

(1) A sole traders' financial statements are private; a company's financial statements are sent to shareholders and may be publicly filed.

(2) Only companies have capital invested into the business.

(3) A sole trader is fully and personally liable for any losses that the business might make; a company's shareholders are not personally liable for any losses that the company might make.

A 1 and 2 only

B 2 and 3 only

C 1 and 3 only

D 1, 2 and 3 **(2 marks)**

19 Which of the following documents should accompany a payment made to a supplier?

A Supplier statement

B Remittance advice

C Purchase invoice **(1 mark)**

20 Goodwill should never be shown on the statement of financial position of a partnership.

Is this statement true or false?

A False

B True **(1 mark)**

21 Which of the following journal entries are correct, according to their narratives?

		Dr $	*Cr* $
1	Suspense account	18,000	
	Rent received account		18,000
	Correction of error in posting $24,000 cash received for rent to the rent received account as $42,000		
2	Share premium account	400,000	
	Share capital account		400,000
	1 for 3 bonus issue on share capital of 1,200,000 50c shares		
3	Trade investment in X	750,000	
	Share capital account		250,000
	Share premium account		500,000
	500,000 50c shares issued at $1.50 per share in exchange for shares in X		

A 1 and 2

B 2 and 3

C 1 only

D 3 only **(2 marks)**

22 The plant and machinery account (at cost) of a business for the year ended 31 December 2005 was as follows:

Plant and machinery – cost

2005		*2005*	
	$		$
1 Jan Balance	240,000	31 March Transfer disposal account	60,000
30 June Cash – purchase of plant	160,000	31 Dec Balance	340,000
	400,000		400,000

The company's policy is to charge depreciation at 20% per year on the straight line basis, with proportionate depreciation in the years of purchase and disposal.

What should be the depreciation charge for the year ended 31 December 2005?

A $68,000

B $64,000

C $61,000

D $55,000 **(2 marks)**

23 Which of the following should appear in a company's statement of changes in equity?

1 Profit for the financial year.

2 Amortisation of capitalised development costs.

3 Surplus on revaluation of non-current assets.

A All three items

B 2 and 3 only

C 1 and 3 only

D 1 and 2 only **(2 marks)**

24 Which of the following statements are correct?

(1) Capitalised development expenditure must be amortised over a period not exceeding five years.

(2) Capitalised development costs are shown in the statement of financial position under the heading of non-current assets.

(3) If certain criteria are met, research expenditure must be recognised as an intangible asset.

A 2 only

B 2 and 3

C 1 only

D 1 and 3 **(2 marks)**

25 A fire on 30 September destroyed some of a company's inventory and its inventory records.

The following information is available.

	$
Inventory 1 September	318,000
Sales for September	612,000
Purchases for September	412,000
Inventory in good condition at 30 September	214,000

Standard gross profit percentage on sales is 25%.

Based on this information, what is the value of the inventory lost?

A $96,000

B $271,000

C $26,400

D $57,000

(2 marks)

26 At 31 December 2004, a company's capital structure was as follows:

	$
Ordinary share capital (500,000 shares of 25c each)	125,000
Share premium account	100,000

In the year ended 31 December 2005 the company made a rights issue of 1 share for every 2 held at $1 per share and this was taken up in full. Later in the year the company made a bonus issue of 1 share for every 5 held, using the share premium account for the purpose.

What was the company's capital structure at 31 December 2005?

	Ordinary share capital	*Share premium account*
	$	$
A	450,000	25,000
B	225,000	250,000
C	225,000	325,000
D	212,500	262,500

(2 marks)

27 The inventory value for the financial statements of Q for the year ended 31 May 2006 was based on an inventory count on 4 June 2006, which gave a total inventory value of $836,200.

Between 31 May and 4 June 2006, the following transactions took place:

	$
Purchases of goods	8,600
Sales of goods (profit margin 30% on sales)	14,000
Goods returned by Q to supplier	700

What adjusted figure should be included in the financial statements for inventories at 31 May 2006?

A $838,100

B $853,900

C $818,500

D $834,300 **(2 marks)**

28 In preparing a company's bank reconciliation statement at March 2006, the following items are causing the difference between the cash book balance and the bank statement balance:

(1) Bank charges $380.

(2) Error by bank $1,000 (cheque incorrectly debited to the account).

(3) Lodgements not credited $4,580.

(4) Outstanding cheques $1,475.

(5) Direct debit $350.

(6) Cheque paid in by the company and dishonoured $400.

Which of these items will require an entry in the cash book?

A 2, 4 and 6

B 1, 5 and 6

C 3, 4 and 5

D 1, 2 and 3 **(2 marks)**

29 At 31 December 2005 the following require inclusion in a company's financial statements:

(1) On 1 January 2005 the company made a loan of $12,000 to an employee, repayable on 1 January 2006, charging interest at 2 per cent per year. On the due date she repaid the loan and paid the whole of the interest due on the loan to that date.

(2) The company has paid insurance $9,000 in 2005, covering the year ending 31 August 2006.

(3) In January 2006 the company received rent from a tenant $4,000 covering the six months to 31 December 2005.

For these items, what total figures should be included in the company's statement of financial position at 31 December 2005?

	Current assets	*Current liabilities*
	$	$
A	10,000	12,240
B	22,240	Nil
C	10,240	Nil
D	16,240	6,000

(2 marks)

30 How should a contingent liability be included in a company's financial statements if the likelihood of a transfer of economic benefits to settle it is remote?

A Disclosed by note with no provision being made

B No disclosure or provision is required **(1 mark)**

31 What of the following material events after the reporting date and before the financial statements are approved are adjusting events?

(1) A valuation of property providing evidence of impairment in value at the reporting date.

(2) Sale of inventory held at the reporting date for less than cost.

(3) Discovery of fraud or error affecting the financial statements.

(4) The insolvency of a customer with a debt owing at the reporting date which is still outstanding.

A 1, 2, 3 and 4

B 1, 2 and 4 only

C 3 and 4 only

D 1, 2 and 3 only **(2 marks)**

32 Alpha received a statement of account from a supplier Beta, showing a balance to be paid of $8,950. Alpha's payables ledger account for Beta shows a balance due to Beta of $4,140.

Investigation reveals the following:

(1) Cash paid to Beta $4,080 has not been allowed for by Beta

(2) Alpha's ledger account has not been adjusted for $40 of cash discount disallowed by Beta.

What discrepancy remains between Alpha's and Beta's records after allowing for these items?

A $690

B $770

C $9,850

D $9,930 **(2 marks)**

33 The business entity concept requires that a business is treated as being separate from its owners.

Is this statement true or false?

A True

B False **(1 mark)**

34 Theta prepares its financial statements for the year to 30 April each year. The company pays rent for its premises quarterly in advance on 1 January, 1 April, 1 July and 1 October each year. The annual rent was $84,000 per year until 30 June 2005. It was increased from that date to $96,000 per year.

What rent expense and end of year prepayment should be included in the financial statements for the year ended 30 April 2006?

	Expense	*Prepayment*
A	$93,000	$8,000
B	$93,000	$16,000
C	$94,000	$8,000
D	$94,000	$16,000

(2 marks)

35 Which of the following items could appear in a company's statement of cash flows?

(1) Surplus on revaluation of non-current assets.

(2) Proceeds of issue of shares.

(3) Proposed dividend.

(4) Dividends received.

A 1 and 2

B 3 and 4

C 1 and 3

D 2 and 4 **(2 marks)**

36 What is the role of the International Financial Reporting Interpretations Committee?

A To create a set of global accounting standards

B To issue guidance on the application of International Financial Reporting Standards

(1 mark)

37 Q's trial balance failed to agree and a suspense account was opened for the difference. Q does not keep receivables and payables control accounts. The following errors were found in Q's accounting records:

(1) In recording an issue of shares at par, cash received of $333,000 was credited to the ordinary share capital account as $330,000.

(2) Cash $2,800 paid for plant repairs was correctly accounted for in the cash book but was credited to the plant asset account.

(3) The petty cash book balance $500 had been omitted from the trial balance.

(4) A cheque for $78,400 paid for the purchase of a motor car was debited to the motor vehicles account as $87,400.

Which of the errors will require an entry to the suspense account to correct them?

A 1, 2 and 4 only

B 1, 2, 3 and 4

C 1 and 4 only

D 2 and 3 only **(2 marks)**

38 Mountain sells goods on credit to Hill. Hill receives a 10% trade discount from Mountain and a further 5% settlement discount if goods are paid for within 14 days. Hill bought goods with a list price of $200,000 from Mountain. Sales tax is at 17.5%.

What amount should be included in Mountain's receivables ledger for this transaction?

A $235,000

B $211,500

C $200,925

D $209,925 **(2 marks)**

39 A computerised accounting system operates using the principle of double entry accounting.

Is this statement true or false?

A False

B True **(1 mark)**

40 A company receives rent from a large number of properties. The total received in the year ended 30 April 2006 was $481,200.

The following were the amounts of rent in advance and in arrears at 30 April 2005 and 2006:

	30 April 2005	*30 April 2006*
	$	$
Rent received in advance	28,700	31,200
Rent in arrears (all subsequently received)	21,200	18,400

What amount of rental income should appear in the company's statement of comprehensive income for the year ended 30 April 2006?

A $486,500

B $460,900

C $501,500

D $475,900 **(2 marks)**

41 Annie is a sole trader who does not keep full accounting records. The following details relate to her transactions with credit customers and suppliers for the year ended 30 June 2006:

	$
Trade receivables, 1 July 2005	130,000
Trade payables, 1 July 2005	60,000
Cash received from customers	686,400
Cash paid to suppliers	302,800
Discounts allowed	1,400
Discounts received	2,960
Contra between payables and receivables ledgers	2,000
Trade receivables, 30 June 2006	181,000
Trade payables, 30 June 2006	84,000

What figure should appear in Annie's income statement for the year ended 30 June 2006 for purchases?

A $331,760

B $740,800

C $283,760

D $330,200

(2 marks)

42 The bookkeeper of Field made the following mistakes:

Discounts allowed $3,840 was credited to the discounts received account.

Discounts received $2,960 was debited to the discounts allowed account.

Which journal entry will correct the errors?

		Dr	*Cr*
A	Discounts allowed	$7,680	
	Discounts received		$5,920
	Suspense account		$1,760
B	Discounts allowed	$880	
	Discounts received	$880	
	Suspense account		$1,760
C	Discounts allowed	$6,800	
	Discounts received		$6,800
D	Discounts allowed	$3,840	
	Discounts received		$2,960
	Suspense account		$880

(2 marks)

43 Which of the following statements are correct?

(1) Materiality means that only items having a physical existence may be recognised as assets.

(2) The substance over form convention means that the legal form of a transaction must always be shown in financial statements even if this differs from the commercial effect.

(3) The money measurement concept is that only items capable of being measured in monetary terms can be recognised in financial statements.

A 2 only

B 1, 2 and 3

C 1 only

D 3 only **(2 marks)**

44 The total of the list of balances in Valley's payables ledger was $438,900 at 30 June 2006. This balance did not agree with Valley's payables ledger control account balance. The following errors were discovered:

1 A contra entry of $980 was recorded in the payables ledger control account, but not in the payables ledger.

2 The total of the purchase returns daybook was undercast by $1,000.

3 An invoice for $4,344 was posted to the supplier's account as $4,434.

What amount should Valley report in its statement of financial position as accounts payable at 30 June 2006?

A $436,830

B $438,010

C $439,790

D $437,830 **(2 marks)**

45 Which of the following statements are correct?

(1) A statement of cash flows prepared using the direct method produces a different figure for operating cash flow from that produced if the indirect method is used.

(2) Rights issues of shares do not feature in statements of cash flows.

(3) A surplus on revaluation of a non-current asset will not appear as an item in a statement of cash flows.

(4) A profit on the sale of a non-current asset will appear as an item under Cash Flows from Investing Activities in a statement of cash flows.

A 1 and 4

B 2 and 3

C 3 only

D 2 and 4 **(2 marks)**

46 **Gareth, a sales tax registered trader purchased a computer for use in his business. The invoice for the computer showed the following costs related to the purchase:**

	$
Computer	890
Additional memory	95
Delivery	10
Installation	20
Maintenance (1 year)	25
	1,040
Sales tax (17.5%)	182
Total	1,222

How much should Gareth capitalise as a non-current asset in relation to the purchase?

A $1,222

B $1,040

C $890

D $1,015 **(2 marks)**

47 **A and B are in partnership sharing profits and losses in the ratio 3:2 respectively. Profit for the year was $86,500. The partners' capital and current account balances at the beginning of the year were as follows:**

	A	*B*
	$	$
Current accounts	5,750CR	1,200CR
Capital accounts	10,000CR	8,000CR

A's drawings during the year were $4,300, and B's were $2,430.

What should A's current account balance be at the end of the year?

A $57,650

B $51,900

C $61,950

D $53,350 **(2 marks)**

48 **What is the correct double entry to record the depreciation charge for a period?**

A DR Depreciation expense
  CR Accumulated depreciation

B DR Accumulated depreciation
  CR Depreciation expense **(1 mark)**

49 A company values its inventory using the first in, first out (FIFO) method. At 1 May 2005 the company had 700 engines in inventory, valued at $190 each.

During the year ended 30 April 2006 the following transactions took place:

2005			
1 July	Purchased	500 engines	at $220 each
1 November	Sold	400 engines	for $160,000
2006			
1 February	Purchased	300 engines	at $230 each
15 April	Sold	250 engines	for $125,000

What is the value of the company's closing inventory of engines at 30 April 2006?

A $188,500

B $195,500

C $166,000

D $106,000 **(2 marks)**

50 A company's motor vehicles at cost account at 30 June 2006 is as follows:

Motor vehicles – cost

	$		$
Balance b/f	35,800	Disposal	12,000
Additions	12,950	Balance c/f	36,750
	48,750		48,750

What opening balance should be included in the following period's trial balance for motor vehicles – cost at 1 July 2006?

A $36,750 DR

B $48,750 DR

C $36,750 CR

D $48,750 CR **(2 marks)**

Section 6

ANSWERS TO PILOT PAPER EXAM QUESTIONS

1 **B**

2 **B**

37,000 + ((517,000 – 37,000) × 5%) – 39,000) = 22,000

3 **C**

4 **A**

5 **B**

–3,860 – 9,160 + 16,690 = 3,670

6 **A**

7 **B**

8 **B**

9 **C**

83,600 + 18,000 – (18,000 × 25%) = 97,100

10 **B**

11 **D**

Receivables ledger control account

	$		$
Opening balance	308,600	Contras	4,600
Credit sales	154,200	Cash received	147,200
Interest charged	2,400	Discounts allowed	1,400
		Bad debts	4,900
		Closing balance	307,100
	465,200		465,200

12 B

1,000,000/40years = 25,000; 1,000,000 – (800,000 – (800,000 × 2% × 10years)) = 360,000

13 B

((300,000 + 30,000)/2 × ½) + (300,000 + 30,000)/2 × 1/3) – (30,000 × ½) = 122,500

14 A

15 D

16 B

17 B

18 C

19 B

20 A

21 D

22 D

(240,000 × 20%) + (6/12 × 160,000 × 20%) – (9/12 × 60,000 × 20%) = 55,000

23 C

24 A

25 D

(318,000 + 412,000 – 214,000) – (612,000 × 75%) = 57,000

26 B

125,000 + (500,000 × ½ × 25c) + (750,000 × 1/5 × 25c) = 225,000; 100,000 + (500,000 × ½ × 75c) – (750,000 × 1/5 × 25c) = 250,000

27 A

836,200 – 8,600 + (14,000 × 70%) + 700 = 838,100

28 B

29 B

12,000 + (12,000 × 2%) + (9,000 × 8/12) + 4,000 = 22,240

30 B

31 A

32 A

(8,950 – 4,080) – (4,140 + 40) = 690

33 A

34 D

(84,000 × 2/12) + (96,000 × 10/12) = 94,000; 96,000 × 2/12 = 16,000

35 D

36 B

37 B

38 D

List price	200,000
Trade discount	(20,000)
	180,000
Sales tax (17.5% × 95% × 180,000)	29,925
	209,925

39 B

40 D

Rent receivable

	$		$
O/Balance	21,200	O/Balance	28,700
Income statement	475,900	Disposal	481,200
C/Balance	31,200	C/Balance	18,400
	528,300		528,300

41 A

Payables ledger

	$		$
Cash paid	302,800	O/balance	60,000
Discounts received	2,960	Purchases	331,760
Contra	2,000		
C/balance	84,000		
	391,760		391,760

42 B

43 D

44 D

438,900 – 980-90 = 437,830

45 C

46 D

890 + 95 + 10 + 20 = 1,015

47 D

5,750 + (86,500 × 3/5) – 4,300 = 53,350

48 A

49 A

(300@230) + (500@220) + (50@190) = 188,500

50 A

Section 7

PRACTICE SIMULATION QUESTIONS

ALL QUESTIONS ARE COMPULSORY

1 Which of the items listed below could appear in a company's statement of cash flows?

(i) Dividends received.

(ii) Bonus issue.

(iii) Irrecoverable debts written off.

(iv) Profit on sale of a fixed asset.

(v) Repayment of loan

A (i), (ii) and (iv)

B (i), (ii) and (iii)

C (i) and (iv)

D (i) and (v) **(2 marks)**

2 The following bank reconciliation has been prepared by the company's bookkeeper as at 31 July 2008:

		$
Overdraft per bank statement		12,700
Add:	Unpresented cheques	13,300
Less:	Lodgements/deposits credited	25,600
Balance per cash book		400

What is the correct balance per the cash book?

A $400 positive

B $25,000 overdraft

C $400 overdraft

D $25,000 positive **(2 marks)**

3 **A company lets out a number of properties. The total rent received in the year ended 31 July 2008 was $810,000. The following amounts were received in advance or were in arrears at the dates shown:**

	31 July 2008	1 August 2007
	$	$
Rent received in advance	33,500	40,800
Rent in arrears (all subsequently received)	35,000	39,200

What amount of rental income should appear in the income statement for the year ended 31 July 2008?

A $813,100

B $809,900

C $810,100

D $806,900 **(2 marks)**

4 **At 31 May 2008, Janet's general ledger included the following balances:**

Trade receivables	$137,850
Allowance for receivables at 1st June 2007	$2,492
Janet's allowance for receivable should be revised to	$2,757

How should receivables be reported on Janet's Statement of Financial Position?

A Current asset of $137,850, Current liability $2,757

B Current asset of $135,093

C Current asset of $137,850, Current liability $2,492

D Current asset of $135,358 **(2 marks)**

5 **When a trade discount is given to a customer the double entry is as follows:**

Dr Discounts allowed

Cr Receivables

Is this statement true or false?

A True

B False **(1 mark)**

6 **On 1 August 2007 Ernie was owed $55,000 by his credit customers. During the year Ernie's credit sales totalled $612,700. Discounts allowed totalled $3,500, Irrecoverable debts $800 and dishonoured cheques amounted to $6,500. On 31 July 2008 Eric was owed $62,550 from his credit customers.**

What was the amount received from credit customers during the year ended 31 July 2008?

A $614,350

B $594,350

C $607,350

D $732,450 **(2 marks)**

7 **Ed's year end is 30 September. He depreciates office furniture at 15% per annum on the straight line basis. A full year's depreciation is charged in the year an asset is purchased, and no depreciation is charged in the year it is sold.**

In March 2005 Ed bought office furniture for $80,000.

If he sells the office furniture for $39,000 in July 2008, what will be Ed's profit or loss on disposal?

A A profit of $7,000

B A loss of $7,000

C A profit of $5,000

D A loss of $5,000 **(2 marks)**

8 **Which of the following statements describes current assets?**

A Assets which are currently located on the business premises

B Assets which are used to conduct the organisation's current business

C Assets which are expected to be converted into cash in the short term

D Assets which are not expected to be converted into cash in the short term **(1 mark)**

9 **Bill uses the first in first out method of inventory valuation. At 1 May 2008 he had 60 units in inventory at a total value of $1,320. The movement on his inventory in May 2008 was:**

Receipts	
14 May	120 units at $22.20
26 May	150 units at $22.30
Sales	
18 May	90 units
28 May	80 units

What is the value of Bill's inventory at 31 May 2008?

A $3,547

B $3,552

C $3,567

D $3,568 **(2 marks)**

10 The following sales tax account has been provided by Claire for the quarter ended 31 December 2008. The account was prepared by an inexperienced book keeper.

Sales Tax $

Bal b/d (amount owing to the tax authority)	22,900	Bank (part payment on account to the tax authority)	10,400
Sales (sales tax element)	387,500	Purchases (sales tax element)	369,000
		Purchases returns (sales tax element)	9,975
		Bal c/d	21,025
	410,400		410,400
Bal b/d	21,025		

What is the correct sales tax balance for the quarter ended 31 December 2008?

A $21,025 debit

B $40,975 credit

C $21,025 credit

D $61,775 credit **(2 marks)**

11 A company had provided income tax for the previous year of $90,000 however it paid income tax of $87,000 this year. At the year-end, the company estimates that $92,000 is owed in relation to income tax for the current year.

What amount will be shown in the income statement account for the current year-end in respect of the income tax?

A $89,000

B $92,000

C $87,000

D None of the above **(2 marks)**

12 Which of the following are features of a spreadsheet?

(i) Look up tables

(ii) "If" statements

(iii) Graphics

(iv) Flexibility

A All the above

B None of the above

C (i), (ii) and (iii)

D (i), (ii) and (iv) **(2 marks)**

13 Pete and Jan are in partnership sharing profits and losses in the ratio 3:2 respectively. Profit for the year was $106,500. Partners' capital and current account balances at the beginning of the year were:

	Pete	Jan
Current account	$15,750 CR	$12,000 CR
Capital account	$10,000 CR	$ 8,000 CR

Pete's drawings were $7,300 and Jan's drawings were $5,500.

What should Pete's current account balance be at the end of the year?

A $79,650

B $72,350

C $82,350

D $86,950 **(2 marks)**

14 Below are the extracts of the trial balance of Caroline, a limited liability company, for the year ended 31 August 2008:

	DR	CR
Plant and machinery cost	$160,000	
Accumulated depreciation		$57,600

The company depreciates plant and machinery at 20% per annum on a reducing balance basis.

The depreciation charge for the year ended 31 August 2008 should be $20,480.

A Yes

B No **(1 mark)**

15 Which of the following are books of prime entry?

(i) Cash book

(ii) Bank statements

(iii) The journal

(iv) Sales returns day book

(v) The general ledger

A All the above

B (i), (ii) and (iii) and (iv)

C (i), (iii) and (iv) and (v)

D (i), (iii) and (iv) **(2 marks)**

16 According to the Framework for the Preparation and Presentation of Financial Statements, how is the measurement of assets and liabilities affected by the application of prudence?

Assets should not be .... Liabilities should not be ....

A overstated understated

B overstated overstated

C understated understated

D understated overstated **(2 marks)**

17 In the year to 30 April 2008, Tanya paid a total of $127,569 to her suppliers.

Her opening and closing balances due to suppliers and her opening and closing inventory values were:

	Opening value	*Closing value*
Suppliers	$11,564	$12,826
Inventory	$5,288	$4,184

What was Tanya's cost of sales for the year to 30 April 2008?

A $125,203

B $126,307

C $127,727

D $129,935 **(2 marks)**

18 Which of the items below would be included in the statement of changes in equity?

(i) Opening balance of the share premium account.

(ii) The profit after tax.

(iii) Dividends proposed after the year end.

(iv) Revaluation surplus.

(v) Issue of shares.

A All the above

B (i), (ii) and (iii) and (iv)

C (i), (ii) and (iv) and (v)

D (i), (iii) and (iv) and (v) **(2 marks)**

19 When Pete's trial balance was extracted, the total of the debit balances was $420 less than the total of the credit balances. He opened a suspense account while he checked the entries. He then found that:

(i) a cash sale for $80 was entered correctly in the cash account, but no entry was made in the sales account;

(ii) when journal entries were posted to the general ledger, a debit entry of $100 was incorrectly recorded as a credit entry of $700.

When Pete corrects these errors what is the balance on his suspense account?

A $300 credit

B $460 credit

C $1,140 debit

D $1,300 debit **(2 marks)**

20 After Toni prepared her draft accounts she discovered that she had incorrectly classified an item of revenue expenditure as capital expenditure.

When the error is corrected, how will her net profit and capital be affected?

	Net profit	*Capital*
A	Increased	Reduced
B	Reduced	Increased
C	Increased	Increased
D	Reduced	Reduced

(2 marks)

21 The International Accounting Standards Council (IASC) is the supervisory body for the regulatory framework of accounting. Its objective is to:

(i) Develop single set of high quality accounting standards.

(ii) Promote use and application of accounting standards.

(iii) Bring the convergence of national and international accounting standards.

A None of the above

B (i) and (ii) only

C (iii) only

D All of the above **(1 mark)**

22 Claude, a limited liability company, has the following building in its financial statements as at 30 June 2008:

Cost	$2,400,000
Accumulated depreciation	$(600,000)
Net book value	$1,800,000

It has been decided to revalue the property to $3,600,000 on 1 July 2008.

What is the double entry to record the above revaluation?

			$
A	Dr	Cost	1,200,000
	Dr	Accumulated depreciation	600,000
	Cr	Revaluation reserve	1,800,000
B	Dr	Cost 1,800,000	
	Cr	Revaluation reserve	1,800,000
C	Dr	Cost 1,200,000	
	Cr	Revaluation reserve	1,200,000
D	Dr	Revaluation reserve	1,800,000
	Cr	Cost 1,200,000	
	Cr	Accumulated depreciation	600,000

(2 marks)

23 At 31 May 2007 Dave's capital balance was $96,578. During the year to 31 May 2008, his drawings were $25,764. At 31 May 2008 his capital balance was $104,864

What was Dave's profit for the year to 31 May 2008?

A $8,286

B $17,478

C $34,050

D $70,814

(2 marks)

24 Which of the following statements are correct?

(i) Under the consistency concept items must always be treated in the same way even if circumstances change.

(ii) According to the money measurement concept only items which can be objectively expressed in monetary terms should be included in the financial statements.

(iii) The prudence concept involves an exercise of caution when making estimates in financial statements. It therefore ensures that assets and income are not overstated and losses and liabilities are not understated.

(iv) According to the materiality concept an item is material if its omission or misstatement might reasonably be expected to influence the economic decisions of the users.

A All of the above

B None of the above

C (i), (ii), (iii)

D (ii), (iii), (iv) **(2 marks)**

25 A company made a profit of $300,000 for the year after charging depreciation of $38,000. During the year it paid off a loan of $75,000, made payments for fixed assets totalling $80,000, issued shares for $100,000 and had an increase in inventories of $8,000.

What will be the increase in cash and bank balances at the end of the year?

A $291,000

B $199,000

C $275,000

D $75,000 **(2 marks)**

26 Hedges, a limited liability company, has an under provision of $5,000 on its tax liability account at end of year ended 31 December 08 before accounting for that year's tax charge.

Estimated tax on profit for the year is $83,000.

What amounts should be shown in the financial statements for year ended 31 Dec 08 in respect of tax?

	Income statement	Statement of Financial Position
A	$83,000	$83,000
B	$88,000	$88,000
C	$88,000	$83,000
D	$78,000	$83,000

(2 marks)

27 **An error of principle entry will result in the disagreement of the trial balance totals.**

Is this statement true or false?

A True

B False **(1 mark)**

28 **A, B and C are in partnership. The profit of the partnership for the year ended 31 July 2007 is $378,000. The partnership agreement provides that the partners are entitled to a salary and interest on capital as follows:**

	Salary	Interest on capital
A	$12,000	$5,000
B	$18,000	$7,000
C	$24,000	$12,000

The profit sharing ratio for A, B and C is 5:4:1. The partnership agreement states that A is entitled to a guaranteed minimum profit share of $170,000. What is the total share of the profits that each partner is entitled to for the year ended 31 July 2007?

	A	B	C
A	$167,000	$145,000	$66,000
B	$170,000	$147,400	$66,600
C	$170,000	$145,000	$66,000
D	$170,000	$142,600	$65,400

(2 marks)

29 **Which of the following statements is correct?**

A Capital expenditure on Research must be capitalised and depreciated as normal

B Dividends proposed after the year end must not be accrued in the accounts

C Contingent liabilities should always be provided in the accounts

D A change in an accounting policy will result in a prior period adjustment **(2 marks)**

30 **Daniel made an error when he calculated the value of his closing inventory, which means that the inventory is overvalued.**

How is his net profit for the year and net assets at the end of the year affected by this error?

	Net profit	Net assets
A	Overstated	Understated
B	Overstated	Overstated
C	Understated	Understated
D	Understated	Overstated

(2 marks)

31 **As per IAS 10 a non–adjusting event which impacts going concern should be adjusted for in the financial statements.**

A True

B False **(1 mark)**

32 Max and Ruby are in partnership sharing profits and losses in the ratio of 2:3. Billy joins the partnership on 1June 2007 and it was decided to make the following changes:

- The profit share ratio is to be revised to 4:4:2.
- Property to be revalued upwards by $100,000.
- Goodwill to be valued at $45,000. It has been decided not to maintain the goodwill account after the admission of Billy.

Max's capital account had a balance of $30,000 credit **before** the above changes.

What is the capital account of Max **after** the above adjustments?

A $70,000 Cr

B $88,000 Cr

C $69,000 Cr

D $30,000 Cr **(2 marks)**

33 Honest Freddie a company has share capital of:

Ordinary Share Capital (75c shares)	$150,000
5% Irredeemable Preference Shares	$75,000

The company pays an interim dividend of 10c per share to ordinary shareholders and the fixed dividend to preference shareholders. The company declares a final dividend prior to the year end of 25c per share to its ordinary shareholders.

What amounts should be shown in the SOCIE and Statement of Financial Position in relation to dividends?

	SOCIE	Statement of Financial Position
A	20,000	23,750
B	23,750	NIL
C	73,750	50,000
D	73,750	53,750

(2 marks)

34 Jane is preparing her bank reconciliation. The bank balance in her general ledger is $422 credit. The only items which need to be dealt with are:

(i) a cheque for $822 issued to a supplier which has not yet appeared on the bank statement;

(ii) interest received of $153 which was credited by the bank, but not recorded by Jane.

What is the closing balance on Jane's bank statement?

A $269 overdrawn

B $1,091 overdrawn

C $553 cash at bank

D $1,397 cash at bank **(2 marks)**

35 Craig, a limited liability company, has the following capital structure:

	$
200,000 Ordinary shares of 50c each	100,000
20,000 20% Irredeemable Preference Shares of $1 each	20,000

The preference shareholders have had their dividend paid during the year.

The following information has been provided for ordinary shareholders:

(i) Dividends declared **before** the year end was 10 cents per share.

(ii) Dividends declared **after** the year end was 15 cents per share.

What are the dividends that should be included in the statement of changes in equity **(SOCIE)** and the Statement of Financial Position for the year ended 31 March 20X7?

	(SOCIE) $	(Statement of Financial Position) $
A	24,000	20,000
B	20,000	20,000
C	50,000	4,000
D	50,000	50,000

(2 marks)

36 Yvette, a limited liability company, has had the following changes in its share capital and loans during the year.

(i) A bonus issue of $35,000.

(ii) A rights issue of $60,000.

(iii) A repayment of $40,000 10% loan notes.

(iv) A receipt of $65,000 8% loan notes.

What amount would appear under the financing activities heading of the statement of cash flows?

A $120,000 net inflow

B $60,000 net inflow

C $25,000 net inflow

D $85,000 net inflow **(2 marks)**

37 During May 2007, Sarah's purchases were $126,500, and her sales were $150,000. Sarah's gross profit is 20% of sales. The value of her inventory at 1 May 2007 was $12,500.

What is the value of Sarah's inventory at 31 May 2007?

A $6,000

B $11,000

C $14,000

D $19,000 **(2 marks)**

38 IAS 2 states that inventory should be valued at the lower of cost and net realisable value.

Which of the following concepts is this in accordance with?

A Accruals

B Prudence

C Going concern

D Matching **(1 mark)**

39 Which of the following errors should be detected by preparing a trial balance?

A A credit entry made on the debit side of the correct account

B A credit entry made on the credit side of the wrong account

C A transaction for which no entries were made

D A transaction entered in the general ledger twice **(1 mark)**

40 In compliance with International Accounting Standards proceeds on sale of non-current assets are found in:

A Statement of Cash Flows

B Statement of Cash Flows and Income Statement account

C Income Statement Account and Statement of Financial Position

D Statement of Changes in Equity and Statement of Financial Position **(2 marks)**

41 Anne has prepared the following reconciliation between the balance on her payables ledger control account in her general ledger and the list of balances from her suppliers ledger:

	$
Balance on payables ledger control account	68,566
Credit balance omitted from list of balances from payables ledger	(127)
	68,439
Undercasting of purchases day book	99
Total of list of balances	68,538

What balance should be reported on Anne's Statement of Financial Position for trade payables?

A $68,439

B $68,538

C $68,566

D $68,665 **(2 marks)**

42 **The Statement of Financial Position of Grass and Trees, a limited liability company, as at 31 December 2007 and 2008 showed proposed dividends declared before the year end of $50,000 and $55,000 respectively. The statement of changes in equity for the year ended 31 December 2008 showed dividends of $100,000.**

How much should be shown in the statement of cash flow of Grass and Trees for the year ended 31 December 2008 relating to the dividends paid?

A $45,000

B $50,000

C $95,000

D $100,000 **(2 marks)**

43 **You are preparing the final accounts for a business. The cost of the items in closing inventory is $41,875. This includes some items which cost $1,960 and which were damaged in transit. You have estimated that it will cost $360 to repair the items, and they can then be sold for $1,200.**

What is the correct inventory valuation for inclusion in the final accounts?

A $39,915

B $40,755

C $41,515

D $42,995 **(2 marks)**

44 **On 1 December 2006 Pat borrowed $40,000 at a fixed rate of interest. A single capital repayment is due on 1 December 2009. During the year to 30 November 2007 the interest of $300 per month has been paid on the last day of each month.**

How should the loan be reported on Pat's Statement of Financial Position at 30 November 2007?

	Current liability	Non-current liability
A	$3,600	$40,000
B	$40,000	$3,600
C	Nil	$40,000
D	$40,000	Nil

(2 marks)

45 While carrying out the reconciliation of the balance on the payables control account in the general ledger with the list of balances from the payables ledger, Celine discovered the following errors:

(i) A payment of $1,700 in full settlement of a balance of $1,714 was correctly recorded on the supplier's account, but only $1,700 was posted to the control account.

(ii) The total of the purchase day book was understated by $900.

(iii) A supplier's credit note was incorrectly recorded in the daybook as an invoice.

(iv) No entries were made to record an arrangement to offset a balance of $620 against balance in the receivables ledger.

Which of the above errors require a correcting entry in the control account?

A (i) and (ii) only

B (ii) and (iii) only

C (iii) and (iv) only

D (i), (ii), (iii) and (iv) **(2 marks)**

46 Andrew's trial balance at 31 October 2008 includes the following balances:

	$
Machinery at cost	85,800
Accumulated depreciation on machinery	21,750
Trade receivables	42,650
Allowance for receivable	1,570
Bank overdraft	6,470
Inventory at 1 November 2007	21,650

His inventory at 31 October 2008 is valued at $22,300

What value should be reported for current assets in Andrew's Statement of Financial Position at 31 October 2008?

A $62,730

B $63,380

C $64,950

D $69,850 **(2 marks)**

47 A trial balance is made up of a list of debit balances and credit balances.

Which of the following statements is correct?

A Every debit balance represents an expense

B Assets are represented by debit balances

C Liabilities are represented by debit balances

D Income is included in the list of debit balances **(2 marks)**

48 Which of the following lists comprises the qualitative characteristics that financial information should possess according to the IASB's Framework for the Preparation and Presentation of Financial Statements?

A Relevance, reliability, comparability, understandability

B Relevance, reliability, prudence, understandability **(1 mark)**

49 After completing his final accounts, Kevin found that he had understated a pre-payment.

How are Kevin's net profit and capital affected by the correction of the error?

	Net profit	Capital
A	Increased	Increased
B	Increased	Decreased
C	Decreased	Increased
D	Decreased	Decreased

(2 marks)

50 At 30 April 2008, Hedwig, a limited liability company, was being sued by an ex-employee for wrongful dismissal. Phoenix has been advised that the claim is 95% likely to succeed, and that damages of $175,000 will be payable if the claim does succeed.

How should this matter be treated in the financial statements of Phoenix for the year ended 30 April 20X8?

A The matter should be ignored

B The matter should be disclosed by note

C A provision should be made for $166,250

D A provision should be made for $175,000 **(2 marks)**

Section 8

ANSWERS TO PRACTICE SIMULATION QUESTIONS

1 D

Dividends received and repayment of loan are cash flows. The rest of the items are non-cash items.

2 C

		$
Overdraft per bank statement		(12,700)
Less:	Unpresented cheques	(13,300)
Add:	Lodgements/deposits credited	25,600
Bank balance per cash book (positive)		(400)

3 A

		$
Total rent received during the year		810,000
Add:	1/8/20X7 rent received in advance	40,800
Less:	31/7/20X8 rent received in advance	33,500
Less:	1/8/20X7 rent in arrears	39,200
Add:	31/7/20X8 rent in arrears	35,000
Total rent receivable for the year ended 31/7/20X8		813,100

4 B

($137,850 – $2,757)

5 B – FALSE

A trade discount is not recorded in the financial statements. The reduced cost of purchase after trade discount is recorded.

6 C

Receivables

Bal b/d	55,000	Discounts allowed	3,500
Dishonoured cheques	6,500	Irrecoverable Debts	800
Credit sales	612,700	Bank (balance)	607,350
		Bal c/d	62,550
	674,200		674,200
Bal b/d	62,550		

7 D

		$
Depreciation (80,000 × 15% × 3 years)	=	36,000
NBV at time of sale (80,000 – 36,000)	=	44,000
Proceeds	=	39,000
Proceeds – NBV	=	(5,000)

8 C

9 C

Closing inventory is 160 units. Using FIFO, 150 of these are deemed to be part of the final delivery, and therefore they are valued at $22.30 per unit = $3,345. The remaining 10 units are deemed to be part of the previous delivery and are therefore valued at $22.20 per unit = $222.

Thus total value is $3,567.

10 B

Sales Tax

Bank (part payment on account to the tax authority)	10,400	Bal b/d	22,900
Purchases (sales tax element)	369,000	Sales (sales tax element)	387,500
		Purchases returns (sales tax element)	9,975
Bal c/d	40,975		
	420,375		420,375
		Bal b/d	40,975

11 A

$92,000

Less: Overprovision of previous year's $3,000

12 A

13 B

Current Account – Pete

Drawings	7,300	Bal b/d	15,750
		Profit Share	63,900
Bal c/d	72,350		
	79,650		79,650
		Bal b/d	72,350

14 A

Plant & machinery	Cost	160,000
	Acc Depn	(57,600)
	NBV	102,400 × 20% = $20,480

15 D

16 A

17 D

Payables

	$		$
Bank	127,569	Bal b/d	11,564
Bal c/d	12,826	Purchases (Balancing figure)	128,831
	140,395		140,395
		Bal b/d	12,826

Opening inventory + Purchases – Closing inventory = Cost of sales

$5,288 + $128,831 – $4,184 = $129,935

18 C

IAS 10 dividends proposed after year end not included in financial statements.

19 A

Suspense a/c

	$		$
Bal b/d	420	Incorrect Jnl entry	800
Cash Sale omitted	80		
Bal c/d	300		
	800		800
		Bal b/d	300

20 D

21 D

22 A

23 C

Closing Capital = Opening Capital + Profit – Drawings

104,864 = 96,578 + 34,050 (Bal fig) – 25,764

24 D

25 C

	$
Profit for the year	300,000
+ Depreciation charges	38,000
– Increase in inventory	(8,000)
– Payments for non current assets	(80,000)
+ Issue of shares	100,000
– repayment of loan	(75,000)
Increase in cash and bank	**275,000**

26 C

27 B

28 D

	A	B	C	Total
	$	$	$	$
Profit for the year				
Salary	12,000	18,000	24,000	54,000
Interest on capital	5,000	7,000	12,000	24,000
Share of profit	150,000	120,000	30,000	**300,000 Bal figure**
	167,000	145,000	66,000	378,000
Guaranteed minimum profit share				
	3,000	(2,400)	(600)	
	170,000	142,600	65,400	

29 B

30 B

31 A

32 A

	Max	Ruby	Billy		Max	Ruby	Billy
Goodwill	18,000	18,000	9,000	Bal b/d	30,000		
				Revaluation	40,000	60,000	–
Bal c/d	70,000	69,000		Goodwill	18,000	27,000	–
				Bal c/d	–	–	9,000
	88,000	87,000	9,000		88,000	87,000	9,000
Bal b/d			9,000	Bal b/d	**70,000**	69,000	

33 C

Ordinary shares $\frac{\$150,000}{75c}$ = 200,000 shares

SOCIE		$
Interim dividend	200,000 shares × 10c	20,000
Final dividend	200,000 shares × 25c	50,000
Preference dividend	$75,000 × 5%	3,750
		73,750
Statement of Financial Position		
Dividend payable		**50,000**

As final dividend is declared prior to year end it is included in Financial Statements.

34 C

Bank

	$		$
Interest Rec'd	153	Bal b/d	422
Bal c/d	269		
	422		422
		Bal b/d	269

	$
Balance per Bank Statement	**553 Bal Fig**
Less: Unpresented cheques	(822)
Balance	(269)

35 A

		SOCIE $
Ordinary Shares	200,000 @ 10c	20,000
Irredeemable Preference Shares	$20,000 × 20%	4,000
		24,000

Statement of Financial Position

Dividends payable Ordinary Shares 200,000 @ 10c $20,000

Dividend declared after year end are excluded from financial statement.

36 D

Bonus issue does not appear in cash flow.

Cash from financing activities

	$
Rights issue	60,000
Receipt 8% loan note	65,000
Payment 10% loan note	(40,000)
	85,000

37 D

		$	
Sales		150,000	100%
Cost of sales			
Opening inventory	12,500		
Purchases	126,500		
Less: Closing inventory	(19,000) **Bal Fig**		
		(120,000)	80%
Gross profit		30,000	20%

38 B

39 A

40 A

41 D

\$68,566 + \$99 = \$68,665

42 C

Statement of cash flows should show dividends paid.

\$50,000 proposed dividend 2007

\$45,000 Interim dividend SOCIE (100,000 – 55,000)

43 B

		$	$
Cost of inventory			41,875
Damaged items:			
	Cost	1,960	
	Expected sale value	1,200	
	Less cost of repairs	360	
	Net realisable value	840	
	Write down ($1,960 – $840)		1,120
	Inventory valuation		40,755

44 C

No current liability since repayment after 12 months and interest is paid monthly within each month.

45 D

46 B

		$
Inventory		22,300
Receivables	42,650	
Allowance for receivables	(1,570)	41,080
		63,380

47 B

48 A

49 A

50 D